A Return to YOU

A Return to YOU

A Journey to Self and Your Greatest Life

Hina Khan

©2024 All Rights Reserved. No portion of this book may be reproduced, stored in a retrieval system, or transmitted in any form or by any means—electronic, mechanical, photocopy, recording, scanning, or other—except for brief quotations in critical reviews or articles without the prior permission of the author.

Published by Game Changer Publishing

Paperback ISBN: 978-1-965653-27-2
Hardcover ISBN: 978-1-965653-28-9
Digital ISBN: 978-1-965653-29-6

www.GameChangerPublishing.com

For my partner, Paul, for your unwavering support and endless cups of tea.

To my boys, Yusef and Imran—I am in absolute awe of you both.

And to you, the reader, for bringing this book to life.

Read This First

Thank you for purchasing and reading my book. As a token of my appreciation, please enjoy this complimentary resource.

Scan the QR Code Here:

A Return to YOU

A Journey to Self and Your Greatest Life

Hina Khan

www.GameChangerPublishing.com

Table of Contents

Introduction – This Book Is Not About Fixing You- You Are Not Broken 1

Chapter 1 – What You Want Is Already Here and Yours- How It Shows Up Is None of Your Business. 9

Chapter 2 – Don't Let Your History Determine Your Destiny - Consciously Creating a New Version of YOU ... 37

Chapter 3 – Having What You Desire NOW by Who You Are BEing 53

Chapter 4 – Change Your Internal Set Points to Match Your Future, Not Your Past 65

Chapter 5 – Making Small External Changes Can Lead to a Big Impact 83

Chapter 6 – Creating Your Inner Circle 95

Chapter 7 – Falling In Love With Your Vessel and Treating It Well 107

Chapter 8 – Creating Mind Blowing Financial Abundance 117

Chapter 9 – You Are the Hero of Your Story 133

Conclusion – This Is the Beginning 137

INTRODUCTION

This Book Is Not About Fixing You~ You Are Not Broken

"It is not who you are that holds you back; it's who you think you're not."
–Denis Waitley, American motivational speaker

Did this book find you, or did you find this book? I wonder about that when it comes to many things, especially books and how they land in our hands. However, this book made its way to you. I want you to know that it's not an accident. You are meant to read this book, and you are meant to read it now.

With that, I want to give you a heartfelt welcome. I am honoured to be with you on this journey as we go through the book together.

I am a former psychotherapist and a peak performance mindset coach. I have been in the world of human behaviour, beliefs, and habits for close to two decades. I love people. I love learning about people and helping people. Over my career, that has happened in many different ways, from TV to psychotherapy to coaching. However, the common throughline is always about helping others. This book is another expression of that. I have not written it for me; it is for you.

This book is about helping you to truly remember who you are. I'm not helping you because you are broken. You're not broken. There's nothing to fix. It is simply about remembering who you are and returning to yourself, to your true, authentic self. I am here to remind you of your divinity so you can claim your destiny.

As you start to read the words on these pages and apply the material, you can expect everything to change. It's like going from living in black and white to vibrant colour. Your relationships will feel deeper, and you will feel connected with those closest to you. Work will feel easy and fun. Money will flow from multiple sources all the time. You will truly be free.

When it comes to freedom, author and speaker Bill Gove put it perfectly when he said, "If I want to be free, I've got to be me. Not the *me* you think I should be. Not the *me* I think my partner thinks I should be. Not the *me* I think my kids think I should be. If I want to be free, I've got to be me, so I better know who I am."

This book is all about you getting to know yourself. When you get to know yourself, you become aware that there is no limit to who you can be, what you can do, and what you can have. You start to see that possibility and opportunity are all there is and that lack and limitation are created.

Imagine being in a state of abundance constantly and consistently. When you have more of what you want, others have more of what they want as well. It's contagious. This book is for those who are really ready to make a shift, to not play small, and to truly claim what they really want.

I imagine that you may have tried this in one form or another and perhaps didn't have the success you had hoped for. Maybe you identified the life you want to have and set things in motion but lost momentum, and the goal fizzled.

Or maybe you were able to attain your goals to some degree, but it was almost like a "one-hit wonder" you had difficulty holding onto. It left as fast as it came in. That is not unusual; it is something most people deal with because there's this one crucial piece missing from the work. It is a piece that most people don't emphasize enough, and that is working on your self-image. That is where we are going to focus. This work we are doing is an inner game, first and foremost. You can have all the strategies in the world, but if you don't have a self-image that matches what you want, it simply won't happen, or it will certainly not last.

I hope this gives you some relief, knowing that if you have struggled or experienced frustration with trying to reach your goals, it's not that you are "bad" at achieving goals or not getting it in some crucial sense. You were simply not given this vital piece of information, which is to raise your self-image to match your goal. I am going to show you exactly how to match the frequency of your goal. We're going to create the version of you (that is actually the true version of you, as you are meant to have all you desire) that is able to create a life you love through ease, joy, and fun. And the best part is, it is about being YOU. Most of us are defending a false identity, and we are going to drop that. That is one thing you will come to realize: Much of this process is about letting go, and we let go to let in. As you let go, you will feel lighter and create space to let in more of what you want. When you do this, you will start to feel free. And being free means feeling at ease, at peace, and joyful. It is the opposite of feeling emotionally drained by worries, which most people are. People are going to bed exhausted from what is weighing on their minds; they have this heaviness that is leaving them tired, yet they can't sleep. They wake up not feeling rested. If that is what it feels like for you, I want you to imagine that that is no longer the case. You wake up refreshed, excited about your day, loving the people you mix with, the work you do, and more.

It means understanding who you truly are and a connection to something beyond you. It means understanding the laws of the universe and trusting your ability to work in harmony with these laws, knowing that no matter what happens externally, you're going to be fine. It's realizing that we are here on this rock that is spinning. It is wild. Earth is wild. This is a pretty wild place, and we're here for such a short time. Let's have so much fun and make an impact in the way that feels right for us. That is what this book is truly about. It is about you creating this version of yourself that has the life you desire. But we're going to do this in a way that is super fun and feels easy.

Now, I do want to talk a little bit about resistance because it is bound to come up. Remember, I said this is about letting go. Well, there may be some beliefs or habits that are not going to go without a fight. They are going to throw everything at you to show you why going for something different is a really bad idea. Why would that happen when this is about improving ourselves and our circumstances? It is because those things that come up cannot exist at your next level. They will have to die, so they are fighting for their lives.

Also, this type of deep dive into yourself can feel selfish because it is all about YOU, and perhaps you have put everyone else before you. It feels uncomfortable to think about yourself and what you would like.

But I want you to know that this is the most generous work you can do. It is generous not only to yourself but also to those closest to you, your community, and the world at large. I have experienced this firsthand. As a result of my own inner work, I've been able to give more money to charities. I've been able to give my family beautiful experiences. I've been able to give random bonuses to my team, and the list goes on and on. I remember hearing that it's not selfish to have what you want; it's selfish to want others to want the same things. When you have what you want, you're going to want everyone else to have what they want. This is the ripple effect of this work you're doing. You will unknowingly become someone's possibility, giving them unconscious permission to get honest with themselves and go for what they really want.

At a conference in Toronto, I heard the renowned Canadian psychiatrist Dr. Gabor Maté say, "The best gift you can give your children is your own happiness." I often share that quote when I am speaking to audiences. Let's give that gift not only to your family but to the whole world!

You're about to enter into the most exhilarating love affair—one with yourself. Please know that I would never ask you or my clients to do anything I have not done. I have embarked on this love affair, and throughout this book, you will hear personal stories from my own journey and examples from my clients. What I share works, and it will work for you—if you let it.

You can expect to see a dramatic difference between the *you* reading this introduction and the *you* who finishes this book. You will be invited to do some exercises. *Do* them to get the full experience of the book. As you do this, you will realize how absolutely incredible you are and that it can only get better and better.

Shall we start your love affair with you?

With love and gratitude, only, always,
–Hina

CHAPTER 1

What You Want Is Already Here and Yours ~ How It Shows Up Is None of Your Business.

"Because creation is finished, what you desire already exists. It is excluded from view because you can see only the contents of your own consciousness."
–Neville Goddard, *The Power of Awareness*

"Creation is finished." I first heard this term through the work of Neville Goddard, and I had no idea what it meant. I didn't understand it; I could not get my head around it. Neville Goddard, if you're telling me that creation is finished, then the thing I would like to create—let's say the amount of money I would love to see in my bank—should be in my bank because it is finished, right? This is what I couldn't get my head around: How was creation finished if I wasn't seeing what I desired in the physical? That is where I was stuck. It was clearly not finished. Oh, and if it is finished, what do I do? I had a lot of questions. You may also have a lot of questions. Well, the good news is that I finally understood it, and I am going to explain it to you! This truly is a life-changing concept, and when you understand and apply it, your whole world changes.

Here we go: Everything that has existed, could exist, or will exist already exists in the present, but it exists in a variety of possible forms. "Creation is finished" means the moment you become aware of something you desire, you have it. I know that is where I got stuck because if I have it, why don't I *have* it, as if it is in my bank account? The fact that everything exists in one form or another means it is here in a different form. It is here in the non-physical, and there is a process it goes through (which we will get to) that brings it into the physical.

So, the claim that creation is finished does not mean that you are dating your dream partner, your dream car is in your driveway, you are living in your dream home, or the money is in the bank. It means that it is *here* in what we would call 4D, and you will see it in 3D through a process. Just because you can't see it in 3D does not mean it is not here.

3D is actually the last part of the manifestation process. When people say, "My [insert desire] has not manifested yet," that is a misunderstanding. It has; it is simply in a different form at the moment.

Think of it this way: Imagine an acorn. What does the acorn have the possibility of becoming? Yes, a tree, and what kind of tree? An oak tree. If you hold an acorn in your hand, the possibility of becoming an oak tree is imprinted on that acorn. But what has to happen first? It must be planted in the right conditions. But the potential is there. This is the same with your dreams and desires: The patterning is within you. If it wasn't, you wouldn't have been able to think of it. And similar to the acorn, it must be planted in the right conditions (the fertile soil of your mind).

Is this making sense now? Are you starting to have an aha moment? It's like an apple. The apple exists in the apple seed. It must be planted in the right soil and tended to. In the beginning, the apple seed and the apple look nothing alike. In fact, it isn't until the very end of the process that the apple looks like the apples we see in grocery stores. For most of the process, as it is "becoming," it looks nothing like the final product. Let's go back to the acorn and oak tree; they look nothing alike. And that's the same with us. We have a patterning within ourselves of something that is bigger and beyond where we are right now. And that patterning, when actualized, looks nothing like us. Well, you may still "look similar" physically, but your thoughts, feelings, and actions will be very different. And as in nature, much of the growth will happen in the dark, underground, and you may question at times if anything is truly happening. I promise you it is.

And that's what you've got to be prepared for. When we're doing this work, when you're creating your audacious goal, you're creating something that you don't know *how* to do, it is beyond your current level of awareness. It is beyond your current self-image. Think about it from the perspective of that acorn again. The oak tree is literally larger than the acorn. It is created that way on purpose (there are no accidents) because the true purpose of a goal is to grow. It is not to get (although getting is fun!). Think about all the growth that is needed to go from an acorn to an oak tree, from the apple seed to the apple. And that growth is happening in the dark, out of sight, underground. That is where the foundation with strong roots is being formed to support the mighty oak tree. Think about all the important work that is being done in that part of the manifestation process. It is important and vital work, and the farmer understands this. We want to understand this for ourselves and our dreams.

Many times, we will abandon our goal because we don't see evidence of it, and due to a misunderstanding and faulty beliefs, we think that means it is not happening or it is not for us. This is why so many people go to their graves with their goals. We want to understand that the final form is the last place it shows up. Our work, then, is to maintain faith even when we don't see "anything," and we do so by understanding that growth happens in the dark. I love what author and change-management expert Price Pritchett says: "Absence of evidence is not evidence of absence." When we don't see it, we will often do the mental equivalent of digging up what we have planted with doubt. Most people abandon their goals. But when you understand this concept that creation is finished, you understand how to work in harmony with the universal laws, which allow you to have faith—but not blind faith, not faith in a vacuum, not faith where you're stumbling along praying, saying, "Oh, Lord, help me. Oh, Lord, I hope this is working," because I really have no idea where you're riddled with doubt.

Faith based on understanding is what I want you to double down on, and that is what you will learn more about in this book. This work is about working in harmony with nature's laws. It is about having the same certainty that when you plant an apple seed, it will result in an apple tree. When you plant your goal and act in harmony with the laws, it will happen; it must happen. You know it in every fibre of your being. You don't question it; you ask, accept, and expect.

And I'm with you every step of the way because just like the oak tree has its patterning in the acorn, you have the patterning of something greater, something bigger, something beyond where you currently are. And just like with the acorn or the apple seed, we have to plant it in the right conditions. That is what we're doing in this book. We're going to show you how to plant what it is that you desire in the fertile soil of your mind. Through faith based on understanding, you are able to water it, feed it, nurture it, and allow the growth that happens in the dark. Then you start to see some of the sprouts, and it's so much fun. You start to see it come into form.

This process is called the "Perpetual Transmutation of Energy." The previous image illustrates how it works: The non-physical manifests through the physical, from "no-thing" moving into "some-thing."

Energy simply exists; it cannot be created or destroyed. This image with the water illustrates that energy merely changes form.

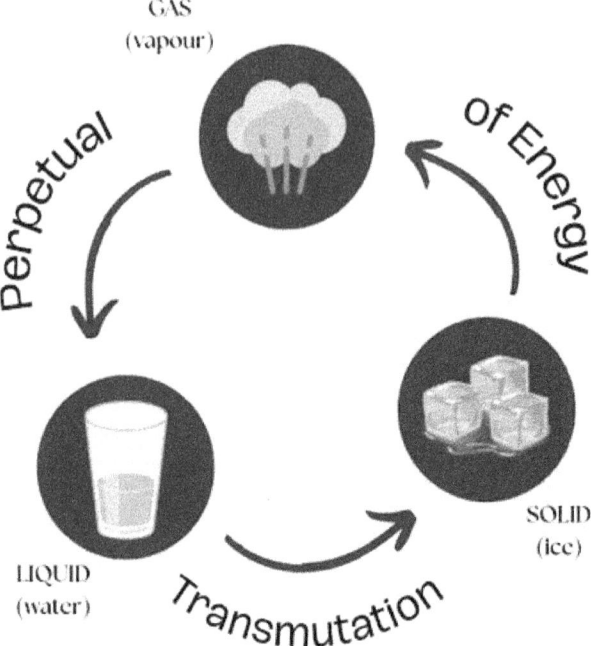

If you were to look around where you are right now, everything you see went through the process of the transmutation of energy. That thing you are looking at came into form, from the non-physical to the physical. It is the same with your ideas. Let's take this book, for example. It was an idea. It was an idea in my imagination, and it came into form through the actions I took. Think of water: You put it in a pot to boil, and as you do this, it turns into steam. It is transmuting.

Now, in our case, we can stop the idea from moving into form by rejecting the idea or having resistance to it. For example, I could have rejected bringing this book into form by saying, "This topic has been covered before," "Who am I to do it?" or "I am too busy." In my case, I accepted the idea and got emotionally involved with it. I could see it (even though I didn't know the title). I imagined receiving notes from people on how this book helped them. I imagined the book launch and more.

With that imagination, I am forming the energy; I am moulding it. This is happening in the subconscious part of my mind, and as I do this, I am emitting a vibration from this frequency that I am tuned into. Let's call it the "Bestselling Book Frequency." From this frequency, I am emitting a corresponding vibration. That vibration is setting up the law of attraction. I am now moving on ideas, taking action from this place. An example of this is finding the publisher and starting to write, etc.

My book is moving to and through me; it is changing form. Think of the book idea as a seed. I planted it in the fertile soil of my mind; the watering and tending to it is the equivalent of me getting emotionally involved with the goal. And, of course, so much of this is happening in the dark as the idea sinks roots and takes hold. This is the process of the perpetual transmutation of energy. So much happens in the dark, and you don't see it, but you've got to stick with it with faith based on understanding. Are you starting to see how the bank account, the person, the car, the dream home, the travel, and the lifestyle are all at the end of this transmutation of energy? Can you see how you've brought energy into physical form? Can you see how it was an idea that you worked with, that you created through your imagination? As you have done that, you are taking it through a process that moves into the physical counterpart of what was imagined. The idea in its physical form is the last piece of the manifestation process.

For much of the process, you are not "seeing" it. My hope is that this has given you some relief as you begin to have an understanding of the process. This understanding has been transformative in the lives of my clients and in my own life.

The purpose of a goal is to grow. And in the creation of that goal, that's where the growth happens. You're not going to grow if you know how to achieve a goal. That's not an audacious goal. You're just doing what you know how to do. What we want to do is create something that we don't know how to do, and that can feel counterintuitive. But that is what is necessary for growth, and this means you have to stretch beyond your current level of thinking and really lean into what you want. What would you want if literally anything was possible? That's your desire. When you land on what that is, the patterning to accomplish it is within you. And similarly to the acorn and the oak tree, it will not look like your current life. You will undergo a transformation.

This can be created through ease, joy, and fun. This is why you can ditch the hard work, the grind, and the struggle—because creating and living the life you love is 95% mindset and only 5% strategy. It's about the inner work first, and then the outer matches the inner. We've got to create the capacity internally.

And this is why the "how" is none of your business. How can you know the how of something that is beyond your current level? Your mind is not able to comprehend all of the ways the "how" can happen. You actually cannot know how. I've got countless, countless examples of this. One example that comes to mind, and this is a very simplistic one, is when I ended up on a private jet with my dear mentor and friend, Bob Proctor. Oh, how I loved that man and feel so blessed that I was able to spend so much time with him, be in his energy, and be in proximity to him. He announced a contest for those in the top 1% of his company (I was in that category) where if you sustained a certain level during a certain period, your name could be picked out of a hat to go on a private jet with him. When I first heard of this contest, I pretended like it didn't matter, and it wasn't important. And then I got honest with myself, and it did matter. I wanted to go on a private jet with Bob. The first step is always telling yourself the truth!

It was approximately two months from that decision to the day when a name would be pulled out of a hat. The first thing I did after I admitted that I wanted this was I accepted the idea and formed it with my imagination. This was difficult at first because I didn't know what the heck happens on a private jet. I didn't know where you go; for example, the airport I would normally go to is Toronto Pearson. Is that the same place that you go to when you fly private? What is the check-in process like? Am I taking off my shoes and dumping my water? I had a lot of questions. Thank goodness we have technology because I could look some things up. Then I had to decide what I could start to visualize that I did not have any resistance to, that I was not fighting to believe or to get emotionally involved in. For me, at the beginning, it was things like having my name pulled out and being announced as the winner to driving to the airport.

Every day, I would visualize these moments and then build on them. I would add more to the scenes in my mind. What I am describing is the perpetual transmutation of energy. Interestingly, I had thought about travelling on a private jet before, but I thought for that to happen, I would have to pay for it, and that felt like something that was way beyond where I was. This is why the "how" is none of your business. When you let go of the "how" but are clear on your desire, the ways will show themselves. Opportunities will appear that you were not even aware of.

As I was getting emotionally involved with the idea of being on the jet with Bob, my body was moving into a vibratory state, and as a result, I was starting to take corresponding action, like blocking off the dates in my calendar for the trip with Bob. Now, when I did this, I didn't tell anybody. I remember my virtual assistant, who has access to my calendar, asking me about it: "Oh, Hina, are you going away on those dates? Will you be doing your calls?"

When she asked me, I was not confident in my answer at all. I answered, "Um, I am not totally sure yet..." And then it happened again with my husband Paul when he noticed it in my calendar and asked me about it. My answer was, "I think I'm going away. Yes, I'm going away. I'm visualizing this thing..."

These external questions showed me that I didn't quite believe it. I didn't confidently say, "Yes, I am going with Bob on his jet to NY." You can see the process is to take the steps even when you don't fully buy it. As I continued to visualize, I did feel more and more like it was mine. My confidence and certainty grew. It got to the point that I knew in every fibre of my being that I was going. There was no shadow of a doubt. I confidently spoke about it to Paul and my VA. In fact, a few days before they announced the winner, I was at a hotel in Orangeville, Ontario, where I was speaking at an event the next day. I wrote a blog post in a Google doc with the title "How I Manifested a Trip on a Private Jet." I wrote the story. It was mine. It was done.

The day came when Bob was going to pull out a name and announce the winner. It was done on FB Live in a private group. I couldn't be there live because I was with a client. When I was done with my session, I opened Facebook on my phone, saw the live, and hit play. Bob was on screen; he said some lovely introductions and then pulled the name out. "The person flying with me is… Carmo!"

Carmo. I was like, *Who the "F" is Carmo? Carmo?* It was so surprising to me because I was like, *This literally doesn't make sense.* I didn't understand it. It was mine, so why was my name not pulled? At that moment, I was so confused.

I texted Paul to let him know, and he asked me how I felt. I told him it didn't make sense to me. I wasn't upset because it felt like a misunderstanding or an error had happened. I simply went about my day. Now, keep in mind that every morning for the past few months, I had been visualizing this. I got up at about 6 a.m., and I wasn't sure what to do. Should I keep visualizing being on the private jet with Bob? Should I not visualize it? I didn't know what to do. In the space of wondering, I had this intuitive nudge: Ask Bob what to do.

I didn't question this nudge; I acted on it immediately. I knew Bob was up early (I learned about a morning routine from him), so I texted him, "Bob, I've been visualizing going to New York with you on your jet. As you know, my name did not get pulled, so my question is, do I continue to visualize being on a private jet with you?" He texted me right back and said, "Yes, Hina, you continue to visualize it. If that is what you want, continue to imagine it happening."

That is exactly what I did. And then another text came in from him, and he said, "You know what? You are exceptional at what you do. You're amazing. The next time I'm going away, I'm going to let Gina know that you're coming with us. You're in Toronto. It's super easy. Do you see how you don't have to concern yourself with the *how*? You created it in a different way."

This is what I love about this work: When you truly let go of the *how* it is often better than you could have anticipated because you are no longer limited in the ways you can imagine it happening. I thought it had to happen in this one way; it happened in a different way that was even better. If my name had been picked that day, I would have been flying with Bob from Toronto to New York (that is a very short flight), but in this other way, I flew with Bob from Toronto to L.A. and got to speak on stage at his event! And here is what I learned about flying private (in case you ever want to do it): You can arrive at the airport 20 minutes before your flight, the pilot checks your passport, and you are not taking off your shoes or dumping your water. And on this particular flight, the snack drawer was really good! I went through all the drawers! When I was on the plane and talking to Bob, he mentioned that he started flying private in his late 70s! He made the change because his time was so valuable to him. He could arrive within half an hour of flying, which gave him more time with his wife and at home. He was not waiting in lines and on the airline schedule. He could decide to fly when it suited him. Flying private made perfect sense to him!

And I'll tell you, it is a lovely way to travel. You're in and out, and then going through customs (because we went through customs on the U.S. side as well) is super, super easy. Cars were waiting to take us to the hotel.

Since that time, I have flown private a few more times, even taking my family! Do you see *how* it's better than you can imagine when you let go of it?

Here's another example that has to do with my family.

Paul and I always knew that we wanted to adopt. We'd already had our first son, Yusef, and we were in the process of adopting our second child. I had no idea what this process was like. It comes with its own set of challenges. We always knew that we wanted this, and we started looking at international adoption. It wasn't coming together; it was hard, and we had been in it for years. It was a complicated process with a lot of uncertainty. A friend who had adopted their children locally told me about something happening in Toronto called the Adoption Resource Exchange (ARE). Now, let me just say that it was also one of those things—I don't know if you've ever felt this way—where it just would not let me go.

I mean, the idea wouldn't let me go. You know when sometimes it feels like this is not working, I just wish the idea would leave me because I don't know what to do. I do not know what to do.

The ARE took place at the Metro Convention Centre in Toronto, and it happens twice a year. It brings together all the Children's Aid Societies and information on the children available for adoption. Before we were going to this event, I had second thoughts and wanted to back out. I actually didn't even want to go. I was tired.

I remember saying to Paul, "Maybe we just don't go. Maybe it's just not meant for us."

Paul was like, "Let's go, and this will be the last thing we do."

So that is what we did. When we arrived, we were given a red binder. In that binder were pictures and information about the children in the foster care system available for adoption. The children's aid agencies representing them were there, like a trade show with booths. Before we went, I asked the universe for a sign if our child was there, and I didn't want to wonder if the sign was a sign. I wanted a hit-you-over-the-head, flashing lights, cannot-be-denied kind of sign.

We looked through the binder. There was a range of children, a range of needs, a range of ages, some siblings, some individuals. It is honestly heartbreaking. As we went through the pages, we came to the end, and I didn't have that feeling until we came to the second to last page. I saw him.

The first thing I noticed was the name Imran, which is one of the names that we were considering naming our child. I looked at Paul, and we just knew. I said, "That's him."

Paul replied, "I know."

I will never forget that moment and his picture. He was 2½ years old, wearing Cookie Monster pyjamas and with the biggest smile. I was in love. And then another feeling comes up right after that—fear.

Has this happened to you? When there is something you truly want, it is right there, and then all of the fearful thoughts come in, like, *What if it doesn't happen?* So much of this (pretty much all of it) is out of our control. *What if there are other people that also feel he is their child?* I felt this so strongly. We took the next step, which was to go to the booth where he was represented, and there we met Jay. Prior to arriving, we wrote a few pages about our family and included pictures. We gave Jay information about us and talked to him. We expressed our interest in Imran, and we were met with a poker face. He was lovely and cordial but neutral.

But then he said that Imran's worker, Trish, would be there in about an hour or so if we wanted to come back. We went for breakfast. I could barely eat; I felt nauseous. My mind was racing as I played out all of these different scenarios. Then we went back and met Trish. Trish was just like Jay. She gave me nothing—there was no sign of hope.

I put my best stuff out there, trying to be the friendliest, nicest person. Nothing, nothing, nothing. I talked about our family, where we lived, and all of these things, and she didn't even crack a smile. Then, when we were leaving, there was a DVD player with a video of the kids, particularly the ones in that booth. Paul said, "Do you want to look at a video of Imran?"

I replied, "Sure, I suppose we can."

We pressed play. And there he was, little Imran. He had a train or a car in his hand, and he was just so cute. He was walking around, and then he hugged a dog. I gasped audibly, so much so that some people turned around. I gasped because the dog he was hugging was the exact same type as the dog we had just gotten one week ago. Here's what you have to understand: My people

(South Asians), there are a few things we did not do. We did not "do" camping, and we did not have dogs as pets growing up in the home. It has changed now with the next generation, but I didn't grow up with dogs.

We never had a dog until one freaking week ago. And it is the exact same dog that Imran is hugging. Now, here's the thing that I didn't know about dogs: when they're a breed, they look exactly alike. Do you want to know what the dog was? A dachshund. Who has friggin' dachshunds?

The wiener dog, black and tan, the exact one that we had at home, is the one that he was hugging in his foster home. That was the hit-me-over-the-head sign I asked for. There was no doubt he was our son. I went back immediately to Trish and said, "Trish, we have the dog. We have the exact same dog." Still nothing from her. Nothing. Now I'm like, *Oh, sweet Jesus. Okay.* So, it's not a cut-and-dried process at all. We submitted the necessary paperwork.

Every time I thought, okay, maybe we're getting closer, there was another curveball. They needed more paperwork. They needed this, they needed that. They needed everything. But here's what I did. I took that picture of Imran from that one sheet and put it in my wallet because, at the time, there was room for two pictures. I had a picture of him, and I had a picture of Yusef. This was all happening behind the scenes. Every time I opened my wallet, I would see my two boys. When I went for a walk with Yusef, I would imagine in my mind that I was holding Imran's hand while holding Yusef's hand in reality. Creation is finished; it's in one form. He is with me in one form. And this is what I would do when I was in the house. I would remember when we told just a few close people, and they would, with the best of intentions, say things like, "Oh my gosh," because it was so up in the air. They'd say, "You know, don't get your hopes up." It was kind of like when you're in your first trimester, and people tell you not to get too attached because you might miscarry. But I was all in. Either it was happening, or it wasn't, and I'd be fully devastated if it didn't. I remember the day Trish and Jay came over to our house for a home visit. Our home had never been as clean as it was that day. We could have put a "For Sale" sign outside and gotten top dollar.

They came over, took a tour of the house, and asked us questions. They met Yusef. When they left, I felt deflated. I said to Paul, "I don't think it went well. I just don't feel it." The rollercoaster of emotions was intense. We had first seen his picture in April, and now it was summer. I was unsure, but Paul reassured me, "You're not auditioning for something. It's not like you weren't happy enough. It was fine. It was really, really good. They were asking great questions and seemed engaged." Still, I had my doubts.

In September, we got a phone call from Jay that he was ours, just shy of his third birthday. This was a reminder that the "how" is none of your business. All those times I thought doors were closing were just redirections, leading us to the right door. All the time I thought we were going to adopt a baby, we ended up with a two-year-old—well, a three-year-old—but we also gained so much more than I could have imagined.

More than a decade later, we are still very close to his foster family, Betty and Luke, who had cared for him from two days ago until he came to our home. We say there are regular folks, and then there are folks like Betty and Luke. They have fostered over a hundred children. I cannot say enough about these people. They are like family to us.

We see them often and celebrate Christmas, holidays, birthdays, and all the special occasions together. We love them dearly. Before Imran's birth mother passed away, we had the opportunity to meet and get to know her. It has been such a beautiful experience. Here he is, my boy. He is my boy. I literally cannot imagine anybody else being my boy as much as if I had given birth to him. The four of us—Paul, Yusef, Imran, and myself—are a family.

You might have something in your heart that won't leave you. And if it looks like it's not happening, it's because that's not what's occurring. It actually is happening.

One thing you want to keep in mind is that when you are going for an audacious goal, something that is beyond your current level, you will challenge your current concept of yourself. And what I mean by that is your worthiness. This is a good thing. We think sometimes that it's not good when all of these negative feelings come up, that that's a sign to not do the thing that we feel we've been called to do or that we want. But it's actually the opposite. It's a sign that you're moving in the right direction.

And it's a sign that you're moving in the right direction because you cannot hold that judgment and have what you desire. The judgment coming up is beautiful because we can then deal with it so that we can have what we desire. Those judgments coming up are like kinks in the hose. I'll give you an example of one of my clients. What she realized in our work together was that her goal, her desire, was to be on various platforms, from podcasts to television to radio and print, sharing her expertise with people. That is what she wanted. She didn't know how, but that's what she really, really wanted. As she admitted this to herself, what came up for her was that taking up space is not safe. She remembered that growing up, it had a negative connotation. It's not something that she should do because, growing up, she was told to keep quiet.

You don't want to brag. You don't want to take the spotlight. It's like if you take the spotlight, you're taking the light off somebody else. Also, this idea of being humble and that a humble and good person does not take up space can be quite conflicting. Imagine someone who wants to take up a lot of space, wants to be out there and wants to be a household name but feels this conflict with deep-seated assumptions about being humble. Well, it's just not going to work. All those feelings are like kinks in a hose. They don't allow the flow. Do you know how a garden hose with a kink slows the water down? That's what happens.

If we allow those judgments to take root, they'll suffocate our goal. They'll crowd it out like weeds. You'll talk yourself out of it in a way that makes you feel like you are right not to go for it. You justify it by saying things like, "I don't really need that; it's not important," or "People who do that are so full of themselves, they're arrogant, they're greedy." We talk ourselves out of it in a way that makes us feel morally superior. Then, we have confirmation bias. We look for evidence to support our judgment, like noticing someone who isn't very nice but is on all those platforms.

What she had to do was work with those judgments and create new beliefs. We reframed it, and she started to realize that she couldn't have the idea, like that patterning within her, like the acorn and the oak tree, if it wasn't possible for her to do, if it wasn't available for her to do. When she is in the spotlight, she lights up other people.

She becomes a possibility for somebody else. She couldn't have this idea if it wasn't available for her to express it.

I'm proud to say that I was on her 100th podcast episode. She has been on national television and has put out products in her field. This is what she has been able to do, and it keeps getting better and better. But you can see how, when you decide what your audacious goal is, what it is that you really want, there will be things that come up that are not a match to it. You've got to override those. Don't let those weeds take over. I hope you're understanding now why it's 95% mindset and 5% strategy. It's all the potential within you, but it's up to you to realize it.

At the end of each chapter, you will be presented with one or more questions to reflect upon. I invite you to grab a notebook and pen and spend some quiet time answering the question(s). This will help you embody and apply the material directly to your life.

REFLECTION (Ask yourself this question):

If absolutely anything were possible, what would I love?

CHAPTER 2

Don't Let Your History Determine Your Destiny ~ Consciously Creating a New Version of YOU

"The 'self-image' is the key to human personality and human behaviour. Change the self-image and you change the personality and the behaviour."
–Dr. Maxwell Maltz, *Psycho-Cybernetics*

In Chapter 1, we really looked at that desire within you: If anything is possible, what would you love? And as you tap into that and we combine it with the understanding of the perpetual transmutation of energy, what we know off the bat is that it is yours.

Creation is finished. It is here now in one form. And now we want to bring it to and through you. And the way that we do that is through changing our consciousness.

Let's start with the current results in your life right now. Many times, we look at our current results and think that they are a reflection of our present: what we have in our bank account, the state of our relationships, our careers, our health, and our lifestyle. This may surprise you, but it is not a reflection of the present. It is a reflection of the past. Think of it this way: When you were at school, you would bring your report card home, and that report card is a reflection of your past. It's what you've done in the past that is showing up in the present, but it is not a reflection of your present because you can already be changing things in the present.

Your current results are a reflection of the past. This is so important to know because so many of us use our history to keep us in the past, and we let our history rule over our destiny. We think, well, that's the way it was, and because it's been like this, *blah, blah, blah, blah, blah*—we allow that to determine what we think we are capable of. This audacious goal that you want to create, this thing that is its own acorn, is going to require a different version of you. I hope this is coming as a relief to you, because it doesn't matter what you've done in the past. I tell my clients, "I don't care about your past, what you have done, what has happened." And that can sound a little callous, but I don't care. I truly don't care what has happened in your past because that is not telling me what is possible for you in the future. It is telling me what your future will look like if you don't make changes in the present.

So, in the present, we can either recreate our past or a version of it, or we can create something completely different. If we go with the latter, it will require a completely different version of you. And this, for me, is so refreshing because I've done some stuff in my past that I actually don't want to repeat. This is where forgiveness comes in: We want to forgive ourselves because we were doing what made sense to us at that time with that level of awareness. Seriously, don't spend any time beating yourself up; show yourself some grace. What you want to understand is your results come from your level of awareness; that's what you were aware of, so that's what you were doing.

But when you're aware of something different, now you have the opportunity to do something different. It is still a choice. It reminds me of when I first had this thought of making my annual income my monthly income. I wasn't aware that that was even a possibility. Like, I didn't even understand that.

You're saying, what I have made in one year, I can make that in a month? The first thing was being aware that that was even a thing, that it was possible. I was aware that money came in a certain cadence. I was not aware that it could come in a different cadence, in a different amount, and in a much shorter amount of time. I became aware of that. Now it is still up to me if I want to accept the idea. But are you getting this? Our results come from our level of awareness.

So don't beat yourself up for things that happened in the past. You weren't aware, but now you are aware of something more, of something different. And when we accept and embody the new awareness, we will see our results change as they match up to that new level of awareness.

Here's another way I want you to think of it. Consider the following diagram:

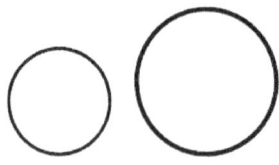

The images are roughly the size of a dime and a quarter. Think of the size of a dime. Think of everything that's happening in your life (the amount of money you make, the state of your relationships, your health, etc.) as being inside that dime because that dime represents your level of awareness.

Now, think about a quarter. Think about how big a quarter is compared to a dime. Now, imagine that quarter represents your expanded level of awareness. Think of everything that would be in that quarter, in that circle, that you could put in there because you have more capacity and are more aware. And here's the beautiful thing: Your awareness keeps growing and growing because it's infinite. It is infinite.

So, this is why the goal is to grow. It is not to get (although the getting is fun) because you're always growing. And when we transition from the physical into the non-physical, we are still expanding because nothing ever dies; we don't die. We just change form. I get so excited about this. I don't know if you can hear me literally screaming or yelling through these pages because we change form, so nothing ever dies. We change form and keep growing and growing.

Okay, I know sometimes I give myself a bit of a headache as I try to get my head around this. But this is why, again, 95% mindset, 5% strategy. You are going to hear me just repeat, repeat, repeat because it's through repetition that you're going to understand this. You will hear it for the hundredth time, and it will click for you.

This is why I am imploring you not to let your history determine your destiny. Please. Look, we've all done things. I've done things that I am embarrassed about, but what happened in the past does not define me. And it doesn't define you.

We have the opportunity to change that if we want something different. What I want you to know is that you're creating your future now by who you are being in the present. Think of it as planting seeds that are going to come up in the future. Think of it as the investment you are making now that will show up in the future. But we have to create the version of you that can have the thing that you desire. It's kind of like if we think of that dime and quarter again, the quarter is bigger, the quarter has a larger capacity. And we do this by creating you. We're literally going to create you through this book; you are creating you.

So, I want you to imagine this audacious goal that you have, something that you don't know how to do but you really, really want. From what we have already learned, we know the goal is done. Let's accept that idea: It is done. From this place, you are not hoping it will happen; it has happened and is simply in a different form right now. Your thoughts are from the place where it is done. An example could be if you want to have a seven-figure business. At this point, most people go to the *how*: how will I do that? And with that question, they are putting distance or a gap between them and their goal. But if we look at it as already being here and already done, now we jump to *who*, not *how*, and the *who* is you. Who do you need to be to have this now? Let's go deeper. What would the thoughts be for the person who has this, for whom it is natural and normal? Another angle is to think about some of your current thoughts and examine them. Would those be the thoughts of someone who is easily generating seven figures in their business? With those thoughts, there would be corresponding feelings. Can you identify them? When many of my clients connect with their audacious goals, some of the feelings they imagine having are peace, joy, and happiness. What would you be thinking, and what would you be feeling?

To bring it into form, you must be that person now. And through the perpetual transmutation of energy, it materializes. We want to be energetically in the future that we have identified, and we want to be in that future in the present. I call this "future-present."

You are writing your own script, and you are the main character. We are going to drill this down throughout the rest of the book, but for now, let's start with some initial thoughts.

The first thing that you can incorporate as a main character in your life is something called "Being My Word" (BMW). It doesn't matter what your goal is; this applies to everyone across the board. If this were the only thing you did, and I mean if you incorporated it and read no further, your life would change. This was a concept taught to me by Steve Hardison, the "Ultimate Coach," and it has become a foundational piece of my work with clients. Fun fact: In my elite group program, Inner Circle, every client receives a beautiful gold bracelet with bees on it to represent BMW.

When Steve explained it to me, he said, "Just imagine that you and I are organizing an event. For the event, we've got some volunteers who are going to come up and help us set up. We're in a room—you can think of a hotel meeting room—and we're going to set up. We are having a meeting with all the volunteers, and there are 20 volunteers.

"We have said we're going to meet at seven in the morning to set up the room. Everybody has said yes. Not one person has said they're not going to meet with us. They've all said yes. Beautiful. We go to bed, wake up, and you and I are in the room at 6:45 a.m. At 6:55 a.m., some people start trickling in to set up, but there are many who have not shown up. So, we split the list of the people who haven't shown up. Let's say 14 people haven't.

"I've got seven people on my list; you've got seven. We are going to phone them. I start phoning some people, and they say, 'Hey, you know, my partner was supposed to wake me up. They didn't wake me up.' Then I go to you, and we're comparing notes, and whatever it is, it's kind of the same thing. Whether they say, 'I'm not feeling well, I slept in, my car couldn't start…,' it's an excuse."

People are making excuses. We do this all the time. We live in a world where people are always making excuses. If you decide that, from the place of your goal, you are a person who keeps their word—whether to yourself or to someone else—that you are someone whose word means something, your word is your bond, and you can trust and rely on yourself, this will create a dramatic difference in your life because it helps with any energetic leaks. You won't have all these people you need to get back to about things or commitments you're trying to get out of because you said yes to something you really wanted to say no to.

When my clients start this, they realize there were things they had said yes to that they would rather say no to. This doesn't mean you have to do everything you said you would, but you should clean it up if you're not going to. If there's something you cannot do or if something comes up, don't leave a person hanging. Tell them right away and tell the truth. I am often asked to do things that are simply not a priority for me, and I graciously decline. I don't have to justify it or give elaborate reasons. Sometimes, we feel that our no is not good enough, that we must have a reason good enough to say no, especially when someone is offering something kind and lovely.

How it also helps you to stop energetic leaks is that many times we will say yes to something because we don't want to say no out of not wanting to hurt somebody's feelings or we don't know how to say no. Between the time that we have said yes and the time that this event is coming up, it's an energetic leak because it is on our mind that we really don't want to go, and we're thinking about how we can get out of it.

How would that change things for you if you simply did the things that you said you were going to do? BMW is part of being in integrity with yourself and others. This is part of the foundational work. We are going to build you from a strong foundation. If you are having trouble keeping your word to yourself and others in one aspect of your life (perhaps your professional life), I can guarantee that it is happening in other areas of your life as well because how you do one thing is how you do everything.

Let's go back to your audacious goal and the version of you that has it.

We want to think about the character traits of the person who has your goal. Now, you might be drawing a blank because it is not something that you can relate to right now. It's okay if you're drawing a blank. What you want to do, then, is think about someone you admire. What are their character traits? Who is the first person that comes to mind, someone you admire and who has the results you want to achieve? Now, consider what you imagine their thoughts are when they wake up.

How do you think they feel?

And with social media, you might actually see some of the actions they take.

When I first started this, one of the things that I wanted was to create a seven-figure business. I had no idea how because doing so would literally make my annual income my monthly income. I had no idea what the habits of people who did it were and what they thought. But then I created a list of people that I admired, and I actually did research and started to listen to podcasts and other things. I actually realized that I knew people who were in that category. And I would start to ask them, when something like this happens, what do you think? What do you think about money? What do you think about sales? What do you think about selling? What do you think about business? All of these things really helped me see the difference between how I was thinking and how the person with my goal would be thinking.

And you know what I realized? They're very neutral and calm and easy. It's their normal. It is natural to do that. So that's what I had to do—create an avatar of this version of me. We want to raise our consciousness to align with the hero image we have of ourselves. There was a method I used that helped me when I encountered resistance. For example, I would say, "I am a seven-figure earner," but then I'd hear a voice in my head saying, *Bullshit, bullshit, you're not.* To help lessen this resistance, I used a tool where I spoke in the third person.

The way that you do this is to write out this version of you in the third person. I had a notebook filled with my hero's image, and I even would write like the hero's image of a seven-figure business owner. You write whatever it is for you: hero's image of [insert yours]. I would write, *"She wakes up, she has a strong morning routine. She does some study, exercises, moves her body, respects her body, and exercises. When she shows up to events, she is put together and polished. She always leaves everybody with the impression of increase* (feeling better from being in your energy). *She has close relationships with her children and her partner."* I literally *wrote* her. *"She always has a minimum of $100,000 in her bank account. Clients love to pay her. She provides* *exceptional value and is worthy of high compensation. She mixes with other millionaires."*

As I am doing this in my mind, my physical situation has not changed; it is very different from what is happening in my imagination. But it is all here in one form or another. This is what I want you to do: First and foremost, you're going to *write* this person. I want you to know that you have a magic pen, and your magic pen's power is that whatever you write happens. Write about this person. What do they drive? Where do they live? How do they show up? What are their relationships like? What are their days like? How do they travel?

When one of my clients adopted this practice, she wrote that she always flew business class. She had been writing this for months! When booking her flight to my retreat in Arizona, she remembered what she had written and decided to book business class. The airline was Air Canada Rouge, where the front of the plane offers nicer amenities, lounge access, and other perks, though it's not quite like a bigger jet with pods. Nevertheless, that's what she booked.

To her delight, the airline changed the plane from a smaller aircraft to a Boeing 777 with pods. Booking a pod seat on this plane would typically cost at least double the price. She had no idea about the change until she boarded the plane. She ended up enjoying four hours in a fully reclined pod, experiencing her new normal.

So, think about it. Who would you be with this magic pen with infinite ink?

As I noted previously, a trick to override resistance is to write out this version of yourself in the third person so your mind doesn't call it unrealistic. For example, instead of *"I have..."* write *"She has..."* When I did this, I wrote in the third person daily for about a week before switching to the first person. Do what feels right for you.

As you do this, remember the principle of perpetual transmutation of energy. Just like a seed planted underground works diligently in the dark to grow, so are you building your foundation.

People still saw me showing up in my minivan, but they didn't know that, in my mind, I was in a different car. Oh, my God, that minivan. You heard it before you saw it; it was so loud. It was absolutely embarrassing. But it was where we were. It was a reflection of the past as we were moving and changing into the physical form. You may have heard and seen my minivan, but I was driving something different. This is a way that we're using our imagination to bring into form what we truly desire, and we are thinking from the goal. You want to have so much fun doing this because you're literally creating yourself.

And that's what we're creating now, being this person now. Because creation is finished, there is a version of you that has the goal that you desire. Remember what we were saying about the perpetual transmutation of energy? It's here. The patterning is within you.

REFLECTION:

What is my audacious goal?

What would it mean for me?

What would I be feeling?

What actions would I take from the place of the goal?

What are some things I would do?

CHAPTER 3

Having What You Desire NOW by Who You Are BEing

"You must first be who you really are and then do what you need to do in order to have what you want."
–Shakti Gawain, *Creative Visualization*

Many times, when we think about what we would love, we think about it from a "when-then" perspective. Like, when I have done this, then I can have that, or when this happens, then I can do this and that. This makes me think of when the family and I were travelling to Australia. It was over March break, and we would be away for a week longer than the scheduled break. I was filling my son's teacher in on the dates we would be away, and his teacher said, "Oh, my gosh, you're going to Australia. My mom has always wanted to go to Australia. She's had a friend there, a really, really good friend she met in university, and she has always wanted to go. She thought she would go when she retired but didn't end up going because it's such a long flight."

That's what I mean: Stop putting your goals off for a better time. There is no better time. All we have is here and now. When you are living this when-then existence, it sets you up for just chasing, chasing, chasing, longing, wanting, as opposed to being and having now. The point of this book and the exercises is to implement the material, embody it, and live it. When we understand that creation is finished and we live from the goal, we are being and having now, and that ends longing. You can start to do things now that are a version of your goal. Energetically, you can start being in the version that you want to be. So many people feel that until they fully have it, they can't do it. Here's another example: One of my clients wanted to move, and she was waiting until she could buy her dream home.

But again, why are we waiting? She was renting, so why not rent in a place that's similar to your dream home, that's close to that, that's even in the neighbourhood that you want to be in? Start there, and then you can start to get into the feeling of it. She did so, which gave her so much clarity that she got into her dream home a lot faster than going from where she was to her dream home. These steps create a bridge to the ultimate goal.

Don't wait until you can do it in its full form before you start to experience it. When you start with where you are, you actually get a lot of clarity. Another one of my clients wanted to have a cleaning team come in. From her ideal self, her future self, she would have a cleaning team come in once a week or once every two weeks. Well, what she could manage now was once a month, so that's what she did!

What can you do *now* that's a version of what you desire? Because then what we're doing is getting onto the vibration of the goal, and it's all vibration. Let me explain it this way. My clients find this analogy really helpful, and I think you will, too. You go to a coffee shop to do some work there. You open up your laptop, you go to your Wi-Fi settings, and you look for the coffee shop's name to join that network. You're not looking for the nail place right beside it or the restaurant on the other side. You want specifically the coffee shop you are in. Why do you want that one? Because the signal is going to be strong, and you have work to do. I want my signal to be the same as my coffee—strong! That's what you tune into. You do your work. Now, when you go home, you open up your laptop, and it auto-joins your home. It's an automatic setting; you don't have to physically do anything.

Imagine that audacious goal is a Wi-Fi setting; it's a frequency. Let's say it's a seven-figure business. That's what I want to tune into. I don't want to tune into a five- or six-figure business. I want to tune into a seven-figure business. And when I tune into that, I am now on the frequency of that. This is what we're doing as you're reading this book and remembering who you are. You're tuning into this frequency. Now, when you get home or into other environments, you may auto-join your past self. What I want you to do is take this Wi-Fi setting with you and always be plugged into it, no matter where you are. I might have been in a minivan, but I was plugged into a setting with a different car. And a quieter one. I might be in my home, but I'm plugged into the frequency of my dream home.

How you'll know if you have auto-joined your past self is if you're responding to things in your current situation from your past self, and also in how you feel. Have you ever been with a group of people and it was so uplifting? Maybe you went to a retreat or an event with really positive people. You leave feeling high, and then you get back into your familiar environments with familiar people, and you start to feel deflated.

What we want is for you to feel that ideal frequency all the time. This is why I value a morning routine and why our **Amplify You™: The Rise** program has helped so many people become incredibly successful. It is because they are in a peak state first thing in the morning and they carry that with them throughout the day.

The goal is for you to be on this frequency all the time. You live, breathe, and eat it, and that's what you see. It's crystal clear. Some of you reading are probably way too young for this, but radios used to have a dial for tuning. If you weren't tuned to a station, you'd hear static—white noise—and as you got closer to a station, you would start to hear a little bit until you hit that sweet spot, and then it was crystal clear. That's what I want you to think about. You're going to drop off it, but the beautiful thing is you'll notice you drop off it. The beautiful thing is that you have something to drop off because what you dropped off from and joined was your previous normal state. But now that's a lower state, a different state. And now you are literally changing your state mentally, emotionally, and physically. And you may think, but Hina, how am I doing that?

I'm still in the same physical body, in the same home, in the same car, and whatnot. To the subconscious, there is no difference between real and imagined. It is all here and now. Imagine that you and I are together. You came over, and we are going to have some sparkling water. I love sparkling water. I take a lemon out of the fridge. I am cutting it, and you're in front of me, watching me cut it into quarters, making these wedges. You're seeing the juice come to the top of the lemon, little droplets, and I hand you one wedge for you to put into your mouth and suck on. As you were imagining this, what happened in your mouth? Most likely, your mouth watered, or saliva formed. Through reading, your physiological state changes through your imagination. That's how powerful it is.

I love what American architect Buckminster Fuller said: "You don't change things by fighting the existing reality. You change things by creating a new model that makes the old model obsolete."

You change things by creating a new model. I'm not standing in front of my minivan saying, "You're not a minivan. You're not a minivan." Do you want to know the new model that you're creating? It's you. You're creating you. You're the new model. We let go of the consciousness of our current model and rise to the consciousness of our goal. And as you do this, again, we're going to hit some edges, and that's what we're going to talk about in the next chapter. Right now, put those characteristics, the hero's image of whatever it is for you, in the first person, in your "I am" statements. I want you to be that person. I want you to tune into that frequency. Describe that frequency. What is life like on that frequency? Feel it to be real in the same way you felt the lemon.

Change your state. Allow this to change your state. It's funny: You're going to have people say things to you like, "There's something different about you. Did you cut your hair? Or did you never wear glasses before, and now you're wearing glasses?"

Because what they're picking up on is a shift in your energy. People are just going to love being around you. Do you know why? Because you love being around you.

Have fun with this. Allow this to be easy, and whenever you feel you have fallen off, that's okay. Just get back to the correct setting to the correct Wi-Fi frequency.

Let me go a little bit deeper into how you know when you have fallen off your hero's image setting. As you're doing this work, you're changing on the inside, but the outside is still the same. Challenges and things that happen externally are still going to be there. But what you want to do is respond to everything from the hero's image that you have created. This is how we are responding from the place of the goal. For example, as you're building this and thinking of this person and the character traits, somebody cuts you off in traffic—how would you respond? It can be as simple as that, like something small like that, or you get the wrong order for something—what would you do? What would you start saying no to that in the outer world you've always said yes to, and now you're going to say no? You see, this is where we start to bump up against things, and why so many people don't want to do this is because they don't want to disappoint people or have people say, "Oh, look at her, she's changed. Who does she think she is? She used to want to do this, and now she doesn't do this anymore." This is really important. This is part of the transformation that's happening: You are responding to things that are in your current circumstances but from a different place, and over time, those things will change.

For example, things that you used to say yes to maybe you don't want to say yes to anymore because you wouldn't from this new frequency. It can even go bigger than that. One of my clients owned multiple locations in the aesthetics industry that were closed during the pandemic lockdown. She responded to that from the place of her goal. Her response was, "The pandemic is happening for me, not to me." It's very different from the way most people approached it, but then she was able to hold on to more than 90% of her employees, and all of her locations opened back up. Many other businesses did not have the same outcome. She shifted who she was being in relation to the situation. You want to do that for everything. Things you used to tolerate that you won't tolerate anymore. Now maybe you'll get some help with things you used to do all by yourself. This is really what it's about: As you're embodying the state of the person who has your goal, you want to respond to everything from that state.

Some questions you could ask yourself when you feel like you have fallen off are: *What would the person with my goals do? How would the person with my goals respond? Would they allow this situation to take them out? Or would they be like, I'm going to take a nap and then get back to it? How would they view things?* This is one of the tangible ways that you can start to feel the difference and that the transformation is happening.

Another personal example is when I was travelling to the U.S. from Canada. This was when they opened up travel and loosened the quarantine requirements, so a lot of people were travelling. The lines were long, and you could feel the frustration. We had to go through U.S. customs, and it was slow going. I could hear people murmuring about missing flights. In fact, I saw someone who was on my flight, and he looked at me and said, "I think we are going to miss our flight."

I responded, "It is all going to work out; we will be on the plane."

Then I made some decisions. One was that I was not going to text Paul and show him a picture of the line. The second was that I was not going to look at my phone because that would show me the time. The third was that I was not going to listen to other people's conversations. I was going to place myself in a bubble and imagine the outcome I wanted. If I were looking at my phone or sending pictures to Paul, I would be getting emotionally involved in doubt and anxiety. As you can see, I wasn't denying that there was a long line; it was slow, and according to my boarding pass, my plane was taking off, but I wasn't participating in it. And because most of the passengers on my flight were in that line, they held the plane, and both my line friend and I made it on!

REFLECTION:

When faced with a challenge (choose a specific challenge in your life), how would the person with my goal respond?

CHAPTER 4

Change Your Internal Set Points to Match Your Future, Not Your Past

"I was always looking outside myself for strength and confidence, but it comes from within. It is there all the time."

–Anna Freud, psychoanalyst

Do you ever feel like you've created a goal, gotten really excited about it, and had all this momentum when you started? It really looks like it's going to happen—things are falling into place, you're meeting the right people, opportunities are happening—and then it kind of fizzles out, and you end up where you usually end up by the end of the year.

If that sounds familiar, you're not alone because that is something that happens to most people, and it has to do with your set point. We all have set points for different areas of our lives: a relationship set point, a financial set point, a health set point, etc. We can definitely see this when it comes to people's relationships with their bodies and weight, dieting, having some success, and then ending up back where they were before, or even gaining more pounds than they lost. Why does this happen?

I want you to think about it like a psychological set point in all these areas. Think of your thermostat setting in your home, for example. I live in Toronto, Canada, and in the winter, we obviously have the heat on. Let's say I've got the heat set at a certain temperature. Then, we're moving some new furniture, so the door is open. What happens at that point? It gets colder in the house. When that happens, it sends a signal that we have dropped from our set point, so the furnace will kick in to bring the temperature back to the designated set point. Once we close the door and are back at the set point, it's not going to go beyond it, either. It will make sure that it stays at that set point. If, for some reason, it's really warm in the house because we're cooking, the mechanism will stay as is because there's nothing for it to do. It will wait until it drops again before moving into action.

I want you to think about this for yourself. Let's say you are thinking about how much you make. If you average out the last few years, you can probably see what your set point is. We'll go further into that in a later chapter. In fact, we're going to go through each area of your life and start to change the set points. But first, I want you to understand what is actually happening, and what is happening is normal.

But we need to override that set point because here's what happens when things start to go well. Gay Hendricks talks about this in his book *The Big Leap*. I've also interviewed him on my podcast in a two-part interview, which I highly recommend you listen to.

In *The Big Leap*, he talks about how we hit this mental edge when things are going well because we are not accustomed to having things go well in our lives. It makes perfect sense. Think about it: You can probably finish this phrase: "It's too good to be true." I don't even know you or what part of the world you're in, but you've probably heard that. Or "The other shoe is going to drop." Or "Don't count your chickens before they hatch." All these fearful beliefs come up when things are going well. One of my clients believed that bad things happened in threes.

Many people have this belief, so when something bad happened, and then something else happened, she would be waiting for the third thing to happen. She was looking for it and wanted to get it over with, like, "Oh, Lord, let that third thing happen so I can just get on with my day." Is this resonating with you?

I'm sure you have also felt this because it's a belief system. We always fall back to our standards, beliefs, and stories. Part of that story for so many of us is that it can't be good. If it's good, it's going to be taken away from us, like the other shoe will drop. When things do become good, we often sabotage them before we feel the inevitable can happen. It's not something we are comfortable with. Losses feel much more powerful than gains because we can measure what we will lose, but we can't measure what we will gain because so much of it is unknown. We're not comfortable with it being good, and we don't necessarily feel worthy of it. We don't feel deserving of it.

It feels different because it is different.

I can have it good in my finances, fine. But can I also have it good in my personal life? I don't know. What about my health? Maybe in all areas of my life?

Now we are stretching it. So I've got to create chaos and complication somewhere in my life so that I can even feel worthy of the good that I do have. I can show people that I know, "Yeah, this is really good, but I want you to know that over here, it's really not that good." Think about it: Even when it comes to vacations, I used to feel that I had to justify it. I would say, "I'm going on vacation. I want you to know that I'm totally burnt out. I'm exhausted. I probably won't even enjoy the first few days." Now I can feel good about going on vacation. Now, I build my calendar around vacations. And it's not even about taking a vacation anymore—it's a way of life. I love to travel; it's not about escaping anything or getting a "break." I love exploring different places, and I love coming home. You're going to reach a point where you're excited to go, and you're excited to come home because all of life is simply good. But you have to create the bandwidth to tolerate all the good. I know it sounds ridiculous, but this is why we see lottery winners lose their winnings within the first few years: it's too much. It's overwhelming for them. They don't have the wealth consciousness to back up the new bank account.

This is what I want you to be super aware of as you read this book. Things are going to start to get better. You're going to start to feel good. You're going to wonder, unconsciously, subconsciously, if you are worthy of that. If you don't deal with that, you will create chaos and complications in your life because you will get yourself back to your set point. Your set point is that it can't be good all the time in all areas of your life. What we want to do is identify it so that we can get ahead of it, and we do that by looking at patterns.

Are there patterns in your relationships where things go well for a certain amount of time, and then a fight starts? Are there patterns in your health? Are you going to the gym, exercising, or moving and drinking water for a certain amount of time, and then you start to take your foot off the gas? Who are the people that you always attract in your life? We want to look at patterns because our patterns, remember, show that the present is a reflection of the past. All of those patterns—what our life looks like—have been created by past thoughts, feelings, and actions. If we want to change that, we need to start filtering it through the person you've started to create in the earlier chapters. Who do you surround yourself with?

Do you always want to be the smartest person in the room?

How do you always end up in the same financial situation at the end of the year, regardless of how you start? Look for patterns. Where do you feel excited about something, and then where does it drop off?

Where do you lose momentum? Where do you start to change your behaviour? This is what we want to do. This is what we want to start to address.

But there's something you need to do to move through this. It's the one thing that will literally change your life. I'm going to keep saying this: You're going to hear this throughout the whole book. There are going to be many "one things" you can choose from. The one thing for this chapter is taking 100% responsibility for your results. I was just on a call this morning, and someone said, "I get so excited about an idea, about something I want to create, and I know I can do it. Then I take it to people close to me, and it's like they burst my bubble. They start to share why perhaps it can't be done, and I lose momentum." I had to be honest with her because that's what makes me really good at my job. I'm not going to tell you what you want to hear. I'm going to change you. I'm going to tell you what's in service of your purpose and your goal. I had to tell her that she was going to these people for validation, approval, and permission. The minute she didn't receive that, it was an out for her.

There's an unconscious commitment to not following through, and that gets played out because it's a pattern. She knows what they're going to do. They're not bad people. They're just responding from their level of awareness. They probably say, "I'm just going to play devil's advocate." If I can just have a moment, I am tired of devil's advocates. I am tired of people saying, "Better be safe than sorry," or "What if this happens?" "What if that happens?" "I just worry about you." Give me angel's advocates. That's what I feel I've created with my community. It's people who are like, "I'm with you. What time do we leave? What do you need? I'm packing. We're there. I don't know how this is all going to end up, but I know that I'm with you either way. If this goes really well, great. If it doesn't, we've learned some things, and we're probably further ahead than we would have been before." Give me angels' advocates, those people who believe in you and your ideas.

I shared this with the person, and then she said, "Yes, but it's my spouse and my mom." It doesn't matter. You have to take 100% responsibility. Are we going to allow other people to dictate what is possible for us? Have you taken your goal to somebody who has done what it is that you want to do? I promise you, you're going to get a very different answer. We want to look at the patterns we create for ourselves that allow us to undo our dreams, and we take 100% responsibility for it.

In these situations, many times, we don't want to do that next step or continue because we're worried about what other people will think. In this case, people are telling you what they think, so you don't even have to try to imagine what it is. But even in the cases where it seems too good to be true, it's like we don't want to offend people by having a good life.

It's as if me doing well in all areas of my life will be offensive to people. It will upset people; it will disturb their equilibrium. Do you know why? Because they will have to look at *themselves*. If *me* having a good life in all areas of my life is going to trigger you, then you will have to be triggered. I refuse to live any other way, and I'm going to take 100% responsibility for that. This is what you want to do (if you wish). You've really got to override people-pleasing. When you think of the person you created in the third person, and now they're in the first person, that version of you is not going to please everybody. I was just talking about this with a client who shared that she wanted to show up more on social media to share what she does. In the past, she received some criticism from colleagues, which stopped her from posting authentically for fear of judgment or being misunderstood by others.

What is interesting about this is that the people she is posting for are not her colleagues. She is posting information for clients, and those clients will be deprived of the knowledge that could help them because of the worry of being judged. She has to make a choice: Either she will be led by what other people think, or she will be led by her mission. I invited her to choose the latter since she invested in my coaching. As long as she was working with me, she should not care what others think and post authentically to her audience and the people she wants to help. When she is done with our coaching program, if she wants to go back to worrying about what others think, she can!

In the meantime, for her and for you, there are people watching you who are so inspired by you, thinking, *Oh my gosh, if they can do it, I can do it.* You're somebody's possibility. You're showing them what is possible for them. This is how you want to start allowing yourself to have more good in your life. You've got to decide first that you want to have more good in your life.

Decide, and these are some things I say to myself: It gets better and better and better. Yes, to this and more. I've acclimatized myself to not putting a cap on how good things can get. Now, you might be looking at me and thinking, *Hina, that's easy enough for you to say.* You're looking at my current results and saying, "Yeah, for sure. You have a seven-figure-plus business. You've got this, you've got that." But I want you to understand that everything I'm asking you to do, even from writing the third person into the first person, I did.

Another piece that was not easy was taking 100% responsibility for my life, for all of my results in every area of my life. I'll give you a personal example. When you grow, which is the purpose of a goal, it feels like another lifetime. I guess it was another lifetime because I'm in a different life now.

I remember waking up and feeling dread. Just dread. I was going to film a TV pilot. I was doing some TV work, and we were shooting a pilot for a show downtown. Paul was taking our three-year-old son to preschool, and I just had such dread. I actually had a dream that night that underneath our bed were a whole bunch of empty alcohol bottles: vodka bottles, whiskey bottles, all sorts of bottles like that. I went and did this audition for the day, but every chance I could, I phoned Paul. I wasn't getting an answer. I phoned his parents. They had tried to get a hold of him and weren't getting an answer either. I just knew something was wrong. He was supposed to pick me up but didn't show up. I felt dread, like a pit in my stomach.

I knew something was wrong. I took public transit (there were no Ubers at the time), and on the bus, I kept phoning Paul's number, dialling it over and over again. It was ringing, ringing, ringing, but there was no answer—until there was. I said, "Paul?"

And they said, "This is the police."

I asked, "What happened?"

Paul had been pulled over for a DUI. I got off the bus, took a taxi (I don't know exactly what happened), and went to where he was. I couldn't even look at him. I was literally sick to my stomach with this. I was just disgusted. Paul then went to his parents' place. It wasn't a quick thing, and he ended up going into an in-treatment program.

You might be wondering, "Hina, what does this have to do with you taking 100% responsibility?" It has to do with me taking 100% responsibility because I knew for years that something was up. Paul would drink in secret; he was a binge drinker, and I knew it and enabled it. I knew on some level, and it was very easy to blame him. I even knew that morning. It would be very easy to put all of the blame on him, and of course, my friends would rally around me, saying, "What a jerk," and all those things. But I was not free from that until I took 100% responsibility.

The responsibility I had to take was that I knew. I also had to decide that I would never, ever let this happen again. Paul did go into treatment, and we separated during that time. I never thought about us getting back together at all. For me, it was done. I thought about the type of person I would want to be with. Here's the thing: I was a match for that version of Paul. I enabled him. But now, through the work we're doing, which I'm taking you through, I had to create a version of me that would not attract that and was not available for that. I had to change from the inside. While I was doing my work, Paul was doing his. Paul truly changed. It's been so beautiful. When we got back together, people would ask, "How do you know this won't happen again?" I don't. But I do know because I take 100% responsibility that if it did, I'm done. I won't pretend like everything's okay. I won't go against my gut. I won't be ashamed of it. I won't feel like I have to hide things to pretend we have this perfect life. That's what I could count on, and that's what it means to take 100% responsibility.

There may be areas in your life where you need to do this. It's part of the AA process of making amends, which I watched Paul do. He called people up, met them, apologized, and asked if there was anything he could do to make it right. That's not easy to do, but that's taking 100% responsibility. When you do that, when I did that, it was freeing for me. Enabling someone else, micromanaging, and managing someone else's life takes a lot of energy (especially when that person is an adult). It was also an excuse for why I couldn't go after what I wanted because there was always chaos and complications with

Paul. There was always something I felt I had to manage and swoop in to be the hero.

It filled something for me, too. You see, I had a set point that things couldn't be that good. I was with someone where it would never be that good because there were always complications. That was my set point: If it was getting good in one area, then there had to be chaos in another area. But when I took 100% responsibility and created the version of me with the life I desired, which is good in all areas, and understood that I'm not responsible for Paul or anybody else, I found freedom. I am responsible to people, my clients, and my family. I am responsible for my children. But Paul is a grown person who is responsible for himself, including his own happiness. He is also not responsible for my happiness. I am responsible for my happiness, and he is responsible for his. I am complete; he is complete. Let's do life together as long as it's fun, not the way we were doing it.

I hope this is landing for you. Maybe there are things you need to clean up for yourself where you haven't been taking 100% responsibility. If you're not going to take 100% responsibility, if you're going to say yes in some areas but not in others, then you might as well close the book now and put it on the shelf or lend it to a friend.

Nothing following in the next few chapters will be worth doing if you're not going to take 100% responsibility for your results and actions. That's what the top 1% do. They take 100% responsibility. In my team, everybody is 100% responsible for their roles. You're not going to find people blaming others. We may highlight things, but we take 100% responsibility.

For example, we had a call where we invited people to our morning calls to get a taste of it. We've done this for years. The wrong link was put out in an email. It went through different eyes and people checking it, but we had to look at it and see where it went wrong. I spoke to the team and said, "These things do happen, but they don't happen to us because we have standards. We're a world-class company, and this can't happen in our organization. I want everybody to look at their part in this." It's not about blaming; it's so we can learn and get better at it so it doesn't happen again. We take 100% responsibility. In my company, we don't blame others. You want this to be your filtering system.

In the following chapters, we're going to create standards for yourself of what you are available for and what you are no longer available for. The way to do that is to get honest with yourself. Are there areas in your life you need to clean up? Remember we talked about "Being My Word."

Is there anything you need to clean up? Is there anything you need to take responsibility for? In the self-image that you're writing, your hero's image, add that you take 100% responsibility for every aspect of your life.

That is the purpose of the hero's image, and now we want to start embodying that so you can see the world through that. The version of you that takes responsibility will be the first step toward creating capacity for you to receive and have what you desire. You will own all of it. That's what I want you to do now.

REFLECTION:

Where am I not taking responsibility for the results in my life?

CHAPTER 5

Making Small External Changes Can Lead to a Big Impact

"Decorating is not about making stage sets; it's not about making pretty pictures for the magazines; it's really about creating a quality of life, a beauty that nourishes the soul."
–Albert Hadley, American interior designer

What we want to do now is start to have the external environment match the internal environment. Think of that hero's image you've created for yourself. You look around and think, *Nothing's really changed externally.* We're going to start changing your physical environment. As I mentioned, we'll go through every aspect of your life. Your current physical environment reflects your old identity. You might look around and realize it doesn't match the person who has your audacious goal. We want to start changing the physical environment to harmonize with that internal environment.

I'm not suggesting you need to sell your home or do a major renovation. Start with simple things. Consider what is the path of least resistance. What is my access point now? What can I get my energy behind? What feels easy? It can be as simple as starting with your bedroom. For example, you could invest in new sheets or a better mattress. I remember when I decided to invest in a better mattress; it was a game-changer for me. Look for easy changes that connect to a feeling that matches your new identity.

Maybe it's time for new pyjamas. My nieces would sometimes laugh because I used to wear Paul's socks, which were bigger and looser. They would laugh at the state of my socks. If you wear socks to bed, consider if they match your new identity. What about your pyjamas? Is it time for a fresh pair? I love to be comfy, so I started investing in nicer quality, comfy pieces. This wasn't all at once but one item at a time, like a hoodie or a pair of leggings. Choose your access point. If you work from home, what is the state of your work environment? Is it a match for the person with your goals?

One of my clients worked from her dining room table, which was cluttered and not conducive to productivity. She created a little nook as her office with a simple table, chair, and fresh flowers. This small change signalled a productive feeling. Remember, the feeling piece is critical. You don't get what you want; you get how you feel about what you want.

You may need to release things that no longer serve you—perhaps some clothing doesn't reflect who you are anymore.

We often hold onto things with a "when-then" mentality, like "when I do this, then I'll wear this." Think of everything as having a purpose now. This is a gradual process; I'm not suggesting a shopping spree. Maybe there are pieces you've kept for sentimental reasons. Do you really need to hold onto them? Much of what we're doing is letting go of things that no longer serve you. Nature abhors a vacuum, so creating space is essential.

If your closet is jam-packed, there's no room for something new. Create space intentionally and meaningfully. Even in my case, letting go of books from my psychotherapy training was challenging because I had invested so much in it. But I realized I wasn't reaching for those books anymore. The knowledge is within me, and I can create space for other things.

As you let go of things, don't rush to fill the space. Acclimatize to having space. This applies to your calendar as well. Many people feel anxious about white space in their calendars. Be comfortable with creating space in your life.

This allows you to bring in meaningful things that harmonize with your hero's identity and elevate your experience. Your identity is made up of all the little, day-to-day decisions.

Making these changes can sometimes feel shallow or unimportant. But think of it as creating standards for yourself. What do you tolerate? I remember coming home after a trip and realizing how organized everything felt in a hotel. We had been debating new closets, and that moment made me realize the importance of an organized space. We called a designer and made changes. It set a new standard for me.

This process can apply to your car, work environment, gym, or any physical space. Look at your environment and identify easy changes. Think of one thing you can add and one thing you can remove. This is a deeper process in my programs, but for now, focus on one small step.

You can even control the environment in your car by listening to podcasts or audiobooks, turning it into a mobile library. The beautiful thing is that you're taking action from your new identity, not habit or autopilot. Look at your environment through the eyes of the person with your goals. You'll see things to let go of and things you want to bring in. Have fun with this process.

Another thing that you can do, which I've done with my clients, is go shopping. *I know I have the best job ever. Do you know why? Because I do it exactly the way I want to do it.* When we go shopping, the rule is that you don't look at the price; you simply look for what you love. The idea is to see what people gravitate toward because, normally, we look at the price first and then decide if we like something. I want people to connect with whether they like something just because it is what it is. How does the material feel? We would see whatever judgments came up because I went through this myself.

Years ago, there was a training in town, and a few people were going shopping afterward. I was invited to go to a luxury department store in Toronto called Holt Renfrew, which has all the high-end brands like Prada, Gucci, and Louis Vuitton. I went with the idea that I was just going to support my friend and not try anything on. Why? Because I created a story that I am not a brand person, brands don't matter to me. I went and watched my friend pick things up. She said, "Why don't you try things?"

I replied, "Oh, no, no, no, it doesn't really matter to me."

She insisted, "But you don't really know that if you don't try it."

She was right. How do I know I don't like brands if I've never tried them?

It was interesting because I felt another pressure: *What if I try something on and then feel obligated to buy it because the sales associate is helping me?* These were all thoughts in my mind that I had to override. Then I tried on a Prada dress. It was probably the first brand-name dress I'd ever tried on. I thought, *Oh my gosh, this is so nice.*

It was something I wouldn't have tried on before, even the style. But wow, the material felt so nice against my skin. The fit was beautiful. You could see the construction. At that moment, I really appreciated the design and detailing. It was gorgeous. I realized: *I guess I do like this.* Then I tried something else from Prada and thought, *Oh, Prada actually suits me. It's really great. It's flattering on me, and I really like it.* I didn't buy anything that day, but it challenged a belief I had.

So that's something else you can do: Go and try things you've denied yourself because you don't feel like you're in a position to purchase them. This can also apply to furniture for your house. It could be going and testing a nice office chair. Have you been working on a kitchen chair or a flimsy chair for the last few years? Do your kids have better chairs than you do at their desks? Really start to go out and try different things to know what you like.

Now, here's the ironic thing about the Prada piece. I assumed, having never shopped for brands like this, that everything started at $10,000—purse, shoes, outfit, everything. When I tried on the dress and looked at the price, it was $2,000. Because of where I thought it was, $2,000 suddenly felt low to me. I still didn't buy it at the time, but it felt low to me because of what I had imagined it would be.

Sometimes, we prevent ourselves from looking at things because we imagine they are out of reach. Find your access point. It doesn't have to be a whole new table; a small nook could be a start. It doesn't have to be a designer outfit, but trying things on gives you information and helps you understand what you like.

It's not about living in a "when-then" mindset, like *When I can renovate, then I'll start changing things.* It can be something simple like a scarf or a nice pair of earrings. It's how you feel about it that matters. This work on your identity changes your story. Over time, what once felt uncomfortable becomes normal.

I can think back to that time with the Prada story. Now, I have many designer clothes and purses, and it's no big deal. It's my normal. Not everything is designer, nor do I desire everything to be. What changed from being scared to try things on and feeling judged to now being normal is the work on my identity. It was about changing the story I was telling myself. And that is freedom.

What's really fun is that the other day, a vendor we work with for our retreats wanted to meet and give me something. We've done many retreats together, and I've referred them to others. She asked if I had time for a coffee, so we met at a business club I belong to. She walked in with a Louis Vuitton bag. For her to have the idea to purchase it and bring it to me, and for me to receive it, shows my capacity to receive.

That's the difference: From not even wanting to try something on to now graciously receiving it as a gift. I want you to see this trajectory. You might be thinking, *What does putting fresh flowers have to do with anything?* But it's about acclimatizing to it, like camping at different heights while climbing a mountain to acclimatize to the thin air.

Even nice candles or a beautiful fragrance can make a difference. Right now, I have a lit candle as I'm writing this, setting up my space and environment to support what I'm doing. I want it to be nice. I have water with me. It could even be the vessel you use for drinking water.

When I host events for my clients, I put my clients in beautiful environments because the setting is important.

One place I often use is the Ritz, where I stay in a specific suite. Clients come, and we spend the day together. When ordering water for the group, I ensure it's in glass bottles, not plastic. I want them to drink from nice glasses. These touches, which my clients might not notice, create an intentional environment that matches the identity they're creating as we birth their dreams in that room.

Even at home, consider what you drink out of. I have a friend who, when she gets something from Starbucks or a coffee shop, pours it into a nice mug.

It could be a nice pen. I'll never forget when my mentor, Bob Proctor, told me to always have a nice pen. I thought, what does it matter? A pen is a pen. But he gifted me a beautiful pen, and it felt different. It doesn't have to be a Mont Blanc; it could be a $10 pen that's just a bit nicer.

I remember being at the bank to send a wire transfer. They offered me their pen, but I used my own. The banker commented on how nice it was. I replied, "Yes, especially when it comes to money; I always sign with a beautiful pen." It's about how you feel. One of my colleagues at an event had a pen with sentimental value but felt better using a nicer pen I had gifted her. These small things may seem inconsequential, but they make up our day. Slowly, this becomes your new normal, or as I like to say, your *now* normal.

It's now normal to use a nice pen or light a nice candle. You might start with a pack of tea lights, and that's fine. Start where you are. I promise you these things will elevate you as you acclimate to a nicer environment and own nice things.

REFLECTION:

What is one thing I can add to my life that will elevate how I feel?

CHAPTER 6

Creating Your Inner Circle

"You are the average of the five people you spend the most time with."
–Jim Rohn, American entrepreneur and motivational speaker.

I'm hoping that you love your environment a little bit more and maybe even made some purchases. You've got some new things in your closet. Look at your life from the lens of that person, that version of you that you've created, and start to bring it into the present. One of the things we want to start with is our relationships.

When I decided that I wanted something different, that I desired more, I knew I would have to change my circle. My current circle was a reflection of the past, and they knew me in a certain way, and I would behave in a certain way around them.

You know, like with siblings. You're grown adults, but you get together—especially if you get together in your family's home or with your parents if they're still alive—and you revert. That's me and my brother. It's like we are immediately goofy teenagers or goofy kids with each other.

So when it comes to your goal, there could be a circle of friends you revert to that you hide from, where you feel like you can't really say what your goal is because they won't get it, as I've mentioned in an earlier chapter. We want to look at this from the perspective of your goal: What do your relationships look like? I want to say this clearly: I am not saying that you are better than anybody. It is simply different levels of awareness.

For example, if you want to learn from someone who speaks that language and has the ability to teach it, you will go where that information is. That's how I want you to think about it with your circle. It's just about going where the awareness is. It doesn't mean that you have to leave people, but you'll naturally start to shift how much time you spend with certain people. Part of this is taking 100% responsibility for your results, not being a people pleaser, and being okay if people don't understand why you are spending time with a different group or doing something else.

Relationships have seasons. Let's face it: There are some people you went to elementary school with that you're no longer friends with because you've outgrown them. There are people you went to high school with that you're no longer friends with. There are people you may have met in post-secondary education or jobs. Sometimes, the connection between us is based on a season in our lives, like school or work. That was what kept the relationship together, so now that you've left, it's not there anymore. It's not that you're better than anybody else; it's just that the season has passed. Then, you're going to have people who are with you throughout all the seasons.

But the frequency with which you may see them will still change. And if a relationship is no longer in service to you, I promise you it's no longer in service to them. You're not doing anybody any favours.

So here's what I had to do. I looked at my relationships and thought, "Okay, what would I love? What do I really want?" I looked at my goal and had to find a circle because my goal was to grow my business, create more impact, and achieve a revenue goal. But I didn't know anybody who was making seven figures. I didn't know anybody thinking about big goals that they didn't know how to achieve, who could accept the idea of making their annual income their monthly income. The first place I went was to listen to podcasts and read books. Then I found my circle of people, and I'm still friends with these people to this day. We created masterminds and a community. That's what my community offers: a place of like-minded people where these types of conversations are normal. It normalizes it. When it's normalized, you also don't have to feel like you need to justify and defend it, which sometimes we feel with people who are at a different level because they don't understand it and have certain judgments around it.

So, from the place of the goal, look at your own relationships. The relationship piece is so important. Think about one of the main concerns we have when it comes to children—who they spend time with.

Why? Because we don't want them to be influenced negatively. How would they be influenced? We know that who you spend time with influences your habits, beliefs, and behaviours. For example, my teenage sons come home saying things we don't say in our house, like "bruh." Paul and I don't use that term. But they come home and start saying it because they've heard it at school. Their friends say it. They say it to each other. We want to make sure our children are around people of a certain mindset so they don't get into trouble because we know they will be influenced. The same goes for us when it comes to our goals. Don't you want to be around people where a million dollars is normal or a million dollars a month is normal? People who are accepting and love talking about their goals?

Because when you are, that's going to rub off on you. It's normal. It's natural. This is why relationships are so important.

Now, let's talk about personal, intimate relationships. Let's go back to Paul and me. Here's the thing: When you have more of what you want, others around you have more of what they want. This might sound odd, but when it comes to Paul, I don't care what he does. I'm going after what I want. I'm creating a life that I love. And I want him to do the same. I remember when I used to enable him and micromanage him. I'm not doing that. I have the freedom to do what I want, and he has the freedom to go after his heart's desires as well. We support each other. I'm not asking him for permission; I ask him for support. He's not asking me for permission; he's asking me for support.

One of the things that often comes up when clients decide to work with me is the fear: What if I grow and my partner doesn't? What if I outgrow my partner? It's like, *Okay, so I am worried that I am going to outgrow my partner, so I will stay where I am, not evolving so that I don't offend them, I don't make them uncomfortable.* This is when you have to take 100% responsibility for your results. You cannot blame your partner for your lack of growth.

The decision rests solely on you. What I have seen more often than not, after working with hundreds and hundreds of people, is that when they start to lean into this, it gives their partner permission to look at what they really want. It's a beautiful thing to take responsibility for your own happiness in the relationship because then you're not being the victim and blaming your partner for why you're not growing. I always say to people, don't ask for permission; ask for support. Just like you would support them in their dreams, you're asking them to support you in yours. You're asking for space to go after what you want, which in turn gives them space to go after what they want.

When it comes to family relationships, maybe there are some text/WhatsApp groups you're involved in that you've got to mute. I'm not saying you have to delete it from your phone, but maybe you mute it or look at it at certain times.

You want to be intentional about who has proximity and access to you.

I remember a time when a colleague texted me asking if I had time to talk. I thought something was wrong, so I dropped what I was doing and got on a call with her. She talked for half an hour, sharing something that was happening with her client, not asking my perspective or any questions, just talking at me and complaining. Afterward, she said, "Thank you, I had to throw that up." I thought, *She saw me as her barf bag!* I realized I was not available to be someone's barf bag. My day, my goals, and what I was working on are not secondary to that. It was a great lesson for me about putting others first. Months later, she reached out again and asked if I had time to talk. I asked her to let me know in a voice note what it was about, and I could get back to her later. She later said, "No, you know what, it's okay, I figured it out." She didn't want to talk; she wanted to vent, and I was not available for that.

So this is what I want you to look at. What groups are still relevant? Many of us have been in groups for so long; maybe we were even in some parent groups that were relevant when our kids were younger but aren't anymore, yet we don't want to offend people by leaving. They're not even going to notice, but we think, *I'm going to stay in this group,* and it's interrupting our days. Maybe there are some neighbourhood groups. One of my clients removed herself from neighbourhood groups that were always complaining about things.

It's like the closet. We are removing things, and we don't have to fill the space immediately. Think about what groups you want to be a part of. What groups are inspiring? What groups would the person with your goal be a part of? What content are you listening to? Reflecting on your hero's image, are there certain shows you used to watch or currently watch that you no longer enjoy? I used to watch a lot of reality shows. In all honesty, I often felt crappy afterward. People were yelling at each other, and these weren't actors—they were real people creating drama. They were flipping tables, yelling, and throwing fists. It didn't feel good afterward; it wasn't a guilty pleasure anymore. I'm not judging anyone who watches these shows because you can also watch them from a different perspective. I'm just sharing where I was at that time. Watching those shows made me feel really crappy afterward.

Remember, when you're bingeing these shows, you're spending hours watching people in unhealthy environments. That's going to affect you. At a certain point, I just couldn't tolerate it anymore. It didn't feel good. I didn't enjoy it. I couldn't watch it. I started watching YouTube videos of interviews with people instead. I love listening to podcasts. You can listen to my podcast, *Possibilities with Hina Khan*. I like to read and study. That became what I binged on. I felt better afterward. I felt my consciousness and awareness growing.

I also looked at who I was following on social media. Was I following people that I actually didn't feel good about? I have to take 100% responsibility for that. I want you to know that you can block people, mute people, and unfollow them. It is your right. Sometimes, I think I have to be the bigger person or that this should not bother me. Well, maybe it shouldn't, but it does. And then, you know, maybe later on, I can unblock or follow them again if I want to.

What you're doing with your relationships and your phone is setting up your own algorithm. Just like with social media, it takes what you spend time on and gives you more and more of that. What do you want to get more of? What would you love to see in your feed? Curate that. Not only will you see it on your phone, but you'll also see it in your life. You'll start to have conversations with people and realize that they are complaining, or you might go back to a family reunion or get together with people from a different season. What's so beautiful about that is you'll see that what used to be normal for you—getting together to complain or talk about a show and spending hours doing that—no longer appeals to you. You can't tolerate that anymore. It just doesn't feel good. You would rather be at home on your own.

You're going to start to see what conversations energize you, where you leave feeling energized and not depleted or like you were someone's emotional dumping ground. It's so beautiful. The relationships you have will be incredible because they will be built on a foundation of abundance and creation, not competition.

So, what I would love for you to do now is get your phone and do an audit. Some of my clients have removed certain apps and games from their phones that weren't adding anything positive to their lives. Look at your phone right now from the identity of the person you have described. Is it a match? Are there some groups that you would like to remove? Are there some podcasts or audiobooks you would like to download?

When you pick up your phone, don't be surprised if you habitually go to certain apps at first because it's all habit. We are creating external cues that match our goals.

What are some books, podcasts, or audiobooks you want to download? So when you're in the car or going for a walk, that's what you're listening to.

We started with the environment, and now we're changing the environment in our minds and our relationships. We're building and building and building.

REFLECTION:

Do an audit: Are there some groups that I have outgrown?

CHAPTER 7

Falling In Love With Your Vessel and Treating It Well

"Health is a relationship between you and your body."
—Terri Guillemets, founder and editor
of The Quote Garden

You know, sometimes I'm just in awe of our physical bodies. It's amazing when you think about it. From our tear ducts to the intricate way our hands function with four fingers and a thumb, every part of our body has a purpose. Our nails, eyes, lips, and tongue—all of these have specific roles. And if you've ever been injured, you really realize the value of your physical body. If you hurt your hand, you suddenly notice how much you rely on it. Without your thumb, even simple tasks become difficult. We often take our bodies for granted, even the incredible things happening when we're sleeping: blood flowing, heart pumping, breathing. It's a miracle.

Consider the way babies come into the world, how we can stand and walk, and the marvel of hormones. Sometimes, it's just wild to think that we are on this spinning planet, walking around, picking things up with our hands. For me, it's wild because we don't think about it often—we're just in these bodies moving about our day. The growth of the body is equally fascinating. Have you ever had a cut and watched it heal itself? A simple paper cut is managed by the body. Think about that. Look in the mirror and appreciate how incredible your eyes, mouth, and ears are. When was the last time you thought about your ears? Look at your hands.

My relationship with my body has changed dramatically by doing this work and thinking about my identity. I look at it from the place of my goal and have changed how I speak about my body. One of the things I incorporated into my self-image, my hero's image, was that I am someone who exercises and moves my body. This decision played into my day-to-day life, influencing not only my exercise routine but also how I speak to myself about my body.

My nieces are now in their 20s, and usually once a year, I'll be with one of them. This year, it'll be with both of them, and we'll have a little aunt-niece time together. It's so much fun. Oh, it's such a great age. And they may say something about their bodies. I will not say anything negative about my body. Now, I won't even say it to myself, but in front of them, I will not say anything negative about my body. It's something that I invite you to think about—this miracle that you are in the body. Maybe you've got some physical limitations, but still, it's a miracle.

When I decided that I was somebody who moved, I made that decision and made it part of my image. I created the habit of going to the gym. The first thing that made it easier for me was working with a personal trainer because they could show me what to do. Since then, I have made better use of my time in the morning. I do my **Amplify You™: The Rise** morning call, and then I go to the gym. I use that time for me, and I'm listening to something— usually not music but personal or professional development, an interview, an audiobook, or something like that. I think of it as me pouring into myself.

The other thing I do is try to be in nature. For me, walking along the water is powerful because there's something about the vibration and energy of water that I find very dynamic. Being among trees or on trails is also important for me. Think about what you can do. If you can't get to a gym, what can you do? What is the access point for you? What would be easy right now? Do you have a pair of walking shoes that you could just use to walk? Think about it from the perspective of your goal. We're thinking about your goal and then matching your self-image and energy to it.

When I looked at relationships, I observed what successful people did, and I found that they exercised consistently. It's clear why: You need to be in a good place physically, which includes sleep and rest, to deliver at the level you want to live at. Exercise and movement are very important for that. They say motion is lotion for your joints and body. My mom went through knee surgery, and many fit people have knee surgeries. When my mom went through it, my brother and I were in the hospital, and we both realized we needed to keep doing squats to avoid it ourselves.

I can tell you that I've never regretted a workout, even when I didn't feel like doing it. What's made it easier is that it's not about judgment. I'm not doing this *in order to* love my body; I do it *because* I love my body. That's an important distinction. I respect and admire every inch of my body. As a result, exercising feels natural. It helps with my mental health and gives me clarity.

Remember, you're not exercising for an external reason. You're exercising because it reflects who you are. Now, let's talk about what you're absorbing into your physical body. Another thing I noticed with my mentors and coaches is that they didn't drink alcohol. I realized I didn't desire it anymore. I may have a cocktail here or there, but I love the feeling of clarity, being awake, and feeling good.

If we go back a few chapters, we discussed how we sabotage things when we're not used to feeling good all the time. I like to feel good all the time, and that self-image affects what I consume. I don't desire sweets or alcohol as much anymore. If I do have a strong craving for it, I have it without judgment.

Think about what you consume and how it makes you feel. In my elite program, Inner Circle, I notice that my clients don't party hard when we meet. Their idea of a party is wrapping up early to get to bed and go for a hike or a walk the next day. They influence each other positively and don't want to feel awful the next day. I see this in my life and with my clients.

For example, I like to get to bed early because I love that time to be with my thoughts. When I mastermind with my colleagues, we plan to get to bed early, meet at the gym in the morning, and start masterminding over breakfast, maybe followed by a massage. I set up my time with my private clients and elite groups this way. We focus on the environment and the pace.

On the note of caring for the physical body, think about any outstanding appointments you may have. When was the last time you had a physical or went to the dentist? Follow up on these things.

Rest is also crucial. Many times, we see rest as a reward after being burnt out. Resting is necessary. Growth happens during rest. If you were training for a marathon, rest days would be part of the strategy. Rest prevents injury and enhances performance.

In your professional life, rest should be part of your strategy. Rest is productive. The more I rest, the more I achieve. Resting can feel stressful because we are not conditioned to it. It can feel uncomfortable, like we're doing something wrong, with shame and guilt tied to it. This stems from a culture of hustle and grind, which is a masculine energy. I'm talking about energetics, not gender. We want to balance the feminine energy of being with the masculine energy of doing.

We've been out of balance, doing too much and not being enough. While you can create results through hustle and grind, it's not fun. I prefer to create a life through ease, joy, and fun, leaning into the feminine energy of rest and allowing it to be part of my strategy.

Consider your environment and give yourself permission to do things that feel easier. Rest is integrated into your life, and with it, you will increase your productivity and effectiveness. Great ideas come when you're relaxed, whether out for a walk, in the shower, or working out. Visualization, writing out your goals, and feeling into them will help you achieve more in less time.

Let me give you an example: Get rid of the nine-to-five antiquated idea of "work" hours and "not-work" hours. What I want you to think about is when you are in flow. For me, I love writing content on a Saturday morning; I'll just sit and have my cup of coffee. The house is quiet, the boys are still sleeping, I've got at least one dog beside me, Paul's doing his own thing, and I really love that time. Many people would be like, "Oh my gosh, you're working on the weekend; you're hustling and grinding." Make no mistake, I am not hustling and grinding. For me, that's when it's easy. Okay, it happens to be on a day that we call Saturday. But that's when it's easy for me. When it does not feel easy for me, it's at three o'clock in the afternoon because I'm more in my zone of genius in the mornings.

The weekends are the best times for me to be writing and doing things. I had to remove any judgment that that was wrong, that I should not be working on the weekend. We want to change the narrative around this. And I also love having a nap on a Thursday at 2 p.m. It's really about tuning in when you are in flow and have no resistance. You're meeting your commitments and obligations but doing so in a way that feels easy. It's about recognizing when you're in flow, rather than focusing on the hustle and grind.

In my signature program, **Amplify You™: The Rise,** we have calls Monday to Friday from 6 a.m. to 7 a.m. EST. I have been doing these calls since March 2020. If it had not come from a place of flow and ease, I would have been burnt out and would have stopped years ago.

It's about achieving more through ease, being receptive, and moving on ideas when they feel right.

REFLECTION:

Look at my calendar.

When are my golden times?

When is the best time for me to work out or be productive?

Create space in my calendar so I have room for spontaneity.

A word of caution: don't fill it up just to feel busy. Productivity is not about being busy. Remove judgment about rest. It's part of the strategy to create your seven-figure business or whatever your goal is. Rest is one of your superpowers. Sometimes, you'll have to force yourself to rest, but think about it from the place of your goal.

CHAPTER 8

Creating Mind Blowing Financial Abundance

"Remember, no more effort is required to aim high in life, to demand abundance and prosperity than is required to accept misery and poverty."
–Napoleon Hill, author of *Think and Grow Rich.*

Sometimes I think people have more trouble talking about money than they do about sex. It could be because we don't really understand what money is. Money is energy. That might sound like a big statement, but it's true. Money is energy; it comes where it is invited and stays where it is welcomed. Since money is energy, it doesn't come from things, although we are often taught to believe that it does. We might think our money comes from our job, business, or clients, but that is simply where money comes through. It can come in through a variety of ways. If you were working at a job and no longer worked there, you would find another vehicle for money to come through.

When we think that money comes from specific things, it can make change hard because we feel like our security is outside of us—in our job or particular situation. The global pandemic showed us that this isn't the case. People who had been in jobs for decades suddenly found themselves unemployed. We must understand that we are the "essential element," as spiritual author Thomas Troward discusses. We should not make something external our source of support. Money does not come from one thing; it comes through things, and it can come through in many ways.

Just the other day, someone won $70 million in the lottery here in Ontario, Canada. They recorded him looking at his bank account for the first time after winning, and the person told him his bank account would look like an international phone number because of all the digits. When he saw his balance, he broke down crying, overwhelmed. Two weeks before, his balance was very different, and now it's $70 million plus. Money is everywhere, and we need to understand what money is so we can learn how to receive it in great quantities.

Receiving is a big part of having more money.

Anytime we want or desire more money, we must increase our capacity to receive. It will be interesting to see if this lottery winner has a wealth consciousness or a poverty consciousness. In a few years, we'll see if he becomes one of the statistics: Most lottery winners return to their base financial point within two years. It's one thing to receive a lot of money, but it's another to have the consciousness to keep it. If he doesn't, he'll go back to his set point.

Most people have a victim relationship with money, which we can hear in their language. They say things like, "Money is tight," "I'm short this month," "I'm paycheck to paycheck," "I can't spend it." We also hear, "Money is the root of all evil," "Money doesn't buy happiness," "Money isn't that important," and "You don't want to be greedy." These statements show how we truly feel about money, which affects our bank accounts. If you want to know how you feel about money, ask yourself: If money were a person in your life, how would you describe that person? I've heard people describe money as unreliable, an asshole, or here today and gone tomorrow.

Be honest with yourself about this. If money were a person in your life, how would you describe it? This will reveal your relationship with money. Wherever you are, we want to make that relationship different. We want money to be your best friend, reliable, always around, supportive, overflowing, welcomed, and invited. Start looking at money as a best friend.

This reminds me of a client from Australia (who I mentioned in a previous chapter). When she first started working with me, she was six figures in debt. Within 18 months, she went from six figures in debt to living in a seven-figure penthouse in Brisbane. She changed her relationship with money and her self-image. As she started to change her relationship with money, she changed her self-image to match her financial goals. She moved out of her old place to a better area, changing how she showed up and who she was. Sometimes, we think we can't do anything until we have fully realized our goal, but we can start taking steps now.

She created a home office, loved where she lived, and was proud of it. Her son used to call their old place "the smelly apartment" because of mould issues. By changing her environment, she elevated how she showed up, what she charged, and the clients she attracted. She would walk to a park across from the penthouse she desired, visualizing and feeling gratitude for living there. In 18 months, she moved into the penthouse with floor-to-ceiling windows overlooking the water. She even had her mom living with her, which was also a goal.

We need to make money our best friend—to invite it into our lives. You won't keep money if you think it's unreliable. You'll create the relationship you feel the strongest about. If it's problematic, chaotic, and confusing, that's what it will be. We need to be honest with ourselves about money without judgment. Look at your finances neutrally. Most people avoid looking at their finances, leaving bills unopened or emails unread.

We need to create money habits, starting with getting honest about what we have. Look at your finances as a reflection of past habits and decisions, not an indicator of what's possible for you. Just think of my client, who was six figures in debt. Take a look at your finances from a neutral perspective, understanding that they represent past habits. Then, start changing them.

One book I recommend is *Profit First* by Mike Michalowicz. It brings order to your mind about money, helping you create a system for your finances. Let's look at your spending habits. How do you feel when spending money? One person I've worked with for over a decade has trouble invoicing. She keeps herself in a poverty consciousness by always feeling poor, even though she has thousands of dollars waiting for her. She's in the habit of not having and creates drama around money.

So she puts off her goods, and it's almost like she doesn't need it. You would think that she doesn't need it, but what she does is keep herself in a stressful state. It's a state she knows, even when she could be keeping herself in a state of overflow and money coming in continually. She's keeping it at arm's length and creating drama around it. One of the things that I always think about is whether there is drama around money. Whenever there is drama around money, whether it's with me or someone else, I bring it to their attention.

A colleague of mine had this issue: I would give her checks, and nine times out of ten, there was a problem with her depositing the check for a variety of reasons. Can you see how there's drama around it? What I want you to ask yourself is, do you have any drama around receiving? Is it hard for people to give you money? Is it complicated? Are you invoicing on time? Do you expect to receive money on time? Do you have a pile of unopened bills?

We want to look at this neutrally and examine our habits. Many people have issues with receiving. They want a seven-figure business but don't feel worthy of it, making it challenging to receive. Whenever there's drama around receiving money, it's not due to a faulty system but because there is trouble receiving on our end. We need to look at why, and many times, it's because people don't feel worthy of it. They don't feel worthy of receiving it, it can feel like it's too much, or they have negative feelings about their ability to manage it.

This often goes back to how money was talked about and treated when you were growing up. Was it a tense conversation? Did you have to ask for money? What was the dynamic with your caregivers around money? In some cases, money was used as manipulation, and there were conditions making a person feel unsafe with money. It will be very hard to receive if you feel that money is unsafe. You won't invoice properly if you feel that money is unsafe. You won't want to talk about it, and you'll be hiding things.

Sometimes I see things on social media that are meant to be funny, but I don't think they are. For example, jokes about women sneaking packages they've ordered past their husbands or paying for things with cash so their husbands don't find out. These jokes reinforce negative beliefs about women and money. That's why I also take issue with terms like "girl bosses" and "boss babes" because they minimize our businesses, which involve money and profits.

Another thing that can keep you in a poverty consciousness is when you start to receive money but have trouble spending it because you're aware of the gap. Instead of keeping it in circulation and spending money on things you would love to buy, you hold onto it because you're very aware of how much has left your bank account.

Whenever there is drama around money, it indicates a problem with receiving. Ask yourself, do you have drama around receiving money? Is it hard for people to give you money? Do you invoice on time? Do you expect to receive money on time?

Many people have issues with receiving because they don't feel worthy of it. They have trouble managing money because of negative feelings. This often stems from how money was treated growing up. If money is a tense topic or used as manipulation, it can make a person feel unsafe with money. If you feel unsafe with money, you won't invoice properly or talk about it.

You can have money but still have a consciousness of poverty. Create a belief system where money is your best friend, reliable, and always here. You are worthy of having the lifestyle you want. It's not just about what's coming in but how you are with money. Do you pay in full or always choose a payment plan? Do you make decisions quickly? When you buy something, do you first look at the price before trying it on?

Think about your language around money. The supply of money is infinite.

A few weeks ago, someone didn't have $70 million in their bank account, and now they do. There is no shortage of supply. You need to create a demand for the supply. If you say things like, "I don't need much," or "I just want enough to be comfortable," that's what you'll get. You can tap into the supply for as little or as much as you want.

Connect to why you want the money. What would you do with it? Would you give bonuses to your team, donate to charities, travel, or create memories with family and friends? These reasons can help you create a demand for money. It's more than the actual cash; it's the psychic income, the psychic increase you receive.

Sometimes, people say you could save money by not spending on things like Starbucks. But there's joy, a "psychic income," from those little luxuries. This joy and increase help you create more. I remember the first bag that felt like a big deal to me was a Michael Kors bag for a few hundred dollars. It was a big deal for me to buy it, and I loved it.

Years later, I replaced it with a Louis Vuitton bag. The jump from a $200 bag to a few thousand dollars was due to my changing self-image.

You need to start with an access point. I couldn't have gone into a Louis Vuitton store initially—even Michael Kors was a stretch. It's how you feel that matters. I love my current bag and have no desire to replace it. This is the psychic income you receive. I also changed my wallet, and I love pulling out money or cards from it.

I remember travelling to Australia for a friend's wedding and buying first-class tickets for my family. It was a stretch, but I did it. Once we were on the plane, it felt natural. It was a great experience, and I decided this was how I wanted to travel from then on.

If there's ever a time you want to do a first-class trip, it's probably this one. I look at the price and remember a video of Steve Harvey talking about this. He says, if you can ever fly first class, do it. Buy a first-class ticket because it literally changes your vibration from the ease you experience from the moment you get to the airport. I did it. I bought those first-class tickets, but I didn't even tell Paul at the time because I was so unsure about it. I didn't want to hear any hesitation or doubt. I was not sure if I should do it. I was telling myself everything like, *Oh, what's the big deal?* The kids were smaller then, so if we had a row of four, we could probably stretch out. *It's all on the same plane; we're going to get there anyway*—for all of the reasons. But I did it. I bought those tickets in November, and we were flying out in March, so I had a lot of time to go back and forth in my mind, questioning what I had done.

I told Paul a couple of months later. He was shocked (in a good way). We didn't tell the boys; we surprised them. I remember walking onto the plane. We're not used to turning left—we're used to turning right to go to economy, to the back of the plane. We turned left, and the boys kept walking around because they thought they had gone the wrong way. They had their little stuffies; it was the cutest thing. Then I said, "No, we're here." Some people had already boarded first class, and they had the biggest smile on their faces because they could clearly tell it was our first time. The boys were like, "Are we here for the whole flight?" I said yes, and they were so excited about flying first class to Australia.

Once you make the decision and you're having the experience of the decision you made, it's like, *Of course. Like, what was I debating?* We had the pods so you could fully stretch out. I remember looking back at Paul, fully stretched out, and I had such gratitude. I was so happy that I could do this. Then, this is what happens. Now you're going to think of ideas like: *This is how I want to travel. I want this to be my normal now. Who would I need to be? What would I need to do?*

I'll never forget when they came by and said, "We're making a cappuccino for your husband. Would you like one?"

I was like, "Yes. Yes, I would."

The little toiletry kit, the snacks that are always available, the ability to eat when you want to eat, being able to stretch out. Then, the whole experience: priority security check-in, the lounge you can use, your luggage coming off first, and you board the plane first. You know how they ask for people to check in their carry-on luggage because the flight is full? You don't have to do that when you're in the front of the plane because there's a designated spot for you.

These are the things I want you to think about while reading this. What is your stretch? What even feels a little selfish? Because it should. It should feel a little like, "Oh, it's just a bit much." What's your "bit much" that you could start to do that you can grow into, expand into, a version of what you desire?

Before I got to the point of buying first-class seats for my family to fly to Australia, I had already been buying the preferred seat, paying for the preferred seat, or paying for premium economy. What can you do to start to put yourself in there so you can have that experience, that psychic increase that happens? What's your "Michael Kors bag," if that's your access point? You want it to feel a little extravagant and indulgent, and that's how you know you're on the right track. It's outside of what you would normally do for yourself, but it's not outside of the version of you that has your goal from that self-image you're creating.

So many times, we treat pleasure, ease, and fun as rewards. I want your life to be the reward. You're not waiting for a special occasion; your life is a special occasion. So wear the dress, break out the nice china, book the massage, buy the tickets. As you do that, you're creating a demand for the infinite supply to flow to you because you're saying, "This is what I'm available for. This is what I expect."

This is why so many of my clients invest in themselves through my elite programs: They want proximity to this energy because having it is powerful. But, of course, it's about finding your access point. Maybe your access point is our entry-level program. Do it. That is perfect because you want to get into a community where these kinds of conversations around money are normal.

When I was aiming for seven figures in my business, I had to be around people where that conversation was normal, where it wasn't a big deal, and where people were achieving it. Through proximity, I learned that they talk differently. They don't say things like, "I can't afford that." They say, "It's just not a priority." They don't talk about numbers as big or small; they're just numbers. It's very neutral. You won't hear things like, "I had a windfall," because it's all very neutral. Money is a reliable tool that amplifies who they are.

I hope this helps you think about your relationship with money. Start by getting honest about where you are with money. Assess your finances neutrally. Eliminate any drama around money. If you have invoices to send, do it. Create a system that makes it easy, even if it means having someone else send the invoices.

When giving and receiving money, do it with gratitude. When I pay my team, I write "with gratitude" in the message. Money is an expression of appreciation. Let's make money *your* best friend. You're entering into a new relationship with money. Set an action plan to build wealth. Understand that money comes through things and think about multiple sources of income.

As you do this, you'll enlarge your capacity to receive.

REFLECTION:

If money was a person in my life, how would I describe that person?

CHAPTER 9

You Are the Hero of Your Story

> *"Personal transformation can and does have global effects. As we go, so goes the world, for the world is us. The revolution that will save the world is ultimately a personal one."*
> —Marianne Williamson, American author and spiritual leader

Well, what a journey we've been on. Now, let's pull it all together in this chapter. You have probably noticed that you feel different and possibly even noticed that your external world is starting to shift to match how you're feeling. You may have noticed that your language has changed, not only what you say out loud but also your inner chatter. You will notice that there are things you would have tolerated in the past that no longer have a place in your new identity. Your whole inner dialogue around your body and finances has shifted. You've literally changed your world by doing this work. I bet you people have noticed. They may say something to you like, "There's something different. I don't know exactly what it is. But I feel like there's something different about you." And there is. There is something wildly different.

This journey is about coming back to who you truly are. It has never been about fixing you because you were never broken. This is about remembering who you are so you can truly reclaim your divinity and claim your destiny. This involves balancing feminine and masculine energy. The feminine energy is about being, and the masculine energy is about doing. We want to have these energies in balance. There's no hustle, grind, or struggle in this work. We want to do this work from a place of relaxation, letting go, and ease, which comes from feminine energy. The actions you take should come from this foundation, not from chaos, conflict, or confusion. They should come from an orderly mind, which is based on the self-image you wrote and the person you've become. This self-image is now your filtering system through which you see the world, like putting on rose-coloured glasses.

We want things to be easy. The idea is that we are not attached to the outcome.

Our work is to stay connected to what we desire, get emotionally involved in it, and drop any resistance to having it.

For example, I was at an event, and the speaker shared his story about going through a divorce. He found the drop-offs and pick-ups for the kids very stressful, and communication with his ex-partner often irritated him. He decided to change his approach, knowing he couldn't control her but could control himself. He decided to create a new relationship with the relationship, calling himself the "Best Ex-Husband Ever." Once he made that decision, he put on those glasses and filtered everything through that energy. Any texts or communications were done with the mindset of being the best ex-husband ever. After eight or nine months, his relationship with his ex-wife had completely changed. One day, she invited him over to meet some friends and introduced him as the "best ex-husband ever." He had literally created that reality.

It is happening, and it is happening at the perfect pace and the perfect time. There will be a gestation period, and touching lightly is also about not being attached to how long it takes. Just know that you're on the right track because you can feel it. And you'll be getting validation from those around you who are noticing something different.

REFLECTION:

What differences have you noticed in your life since applying this material?

CONCLUSION

This Is the Beginning

"And suddenly, you know. It is time to start something new and trust the magic of beginnings."
—Meister Eckhart, German theologian and mystic

I want to start by saying thank you. Thank you for investing your time and resources in yourself to go on this wonderful journey. At the beginning of the book, I called it a love affair with yourself. I hope you've truly fallen in love with yourself, recognize how extraordinary you are, and understand that this is just the beginning.

From here, with this foundation, it simply gets better and better. That's the beautiful thing. You know, I used to get so annoyed when people would say the journey is the manifestation. I would think, *I want the thing. I'm good. Yes, I've had enough of the journey.* But when you understand the laws of the universe and what we have talked about, the journey is the manifestation. It is so much fun. The people you meet and the types of things you do are becoming *your* normal because you're taking risks and trying different things from this new self-image. I am so excited for you, and I don't want it to end here.

I would love to continue working with you, and there are a few different ways we can do that. You could also join one of our programs. We have many different access points for you. This is for you if you're ready to apply this material in a heightened and elevated way and if you'd like to have some accountability and feel supported every step of the way. We've got you. We are with you every step of the way.

So, for me, this is not goodbye; this is not the end. Now, we just move on to another platform, and it is just the beginning. I'll see you over there.

THANK YOU FOR BRINGING THIS BOOK TO LIFE!

Please enjoy this complimentary bonus!

SCAN THE QR CODE:

I appreciate your interest in my book and value your feedback as it helps me improve future versions of this book. I would appreciate it if you could leave your invaluable review on Amazon.com with your feedback. Thank you!

www.ingramcontent.com/pod-product-compliance
Lightning Source LLC
LaVergne TN
LVHW041337080426
835512LV00006B/502